YESTER
DAY,
TODAY
&FOR
EVER

YESTER DAY, TODAY & FOR EVER

a journey through

30 unchangeable promises

from the mouth of God

EUGENE LUNING

DESTINY IMAGE® PUBLISHERS, INC.
P.O. Box 310, Shippensburg, PA 17257-0310
"Promoting Inspired Lives."

This book and all other Destiny Image and Destiny Image Fiction books are available at Christian bookstores and distributors worldwide.

Cover design by: Christian Rafetto

For more information on foreign distributors, call 717-532-3040.

Reach us on the Internet: www.destinyimage.com.

ISBN 13 TP: 978-0-7684-5697-4

ISBN 13 eBook: 978-0-7684-5698-1

For Worldwide Distribution, Printed in the U.S.A.

1 2 3 4 5 6 7 8 / 24 23 22 21 20

"Jesus Christ is the same yesterday and today and forever."

—Hebrews 13:8

*   *   *   *   *   *   *

"When the habit of inwardly gazing Godward becomes fixed within us we shall be ushered onto a new level of spiritual life more in keeping with the promises of God and the mood of the New Testament. The Triune God will be our dwelling place even while our feet walk the low road of simple duty here among men."

—A.W. Tozer, The Pursuit of God

To Jenny.

CONTENTS

PROLOGUE

If you are reading these words near the date of their original publication, then you're perfectly familiar with the feeling of the time in which they were written: approximately the one-month point of the sheltered-in-place, locked-down, quarantined, national crisis that resulted from the novel coronavirus, COVID-19. On the night when it first became clear that everything was changing—when the markets continued to be all over the place, when schools and churches were first announcing long-term closures—my son, Tripp, and I went to the store, and I could tell that both of us, father and son, were quietly observing the realities of the twin atmospheres of uncertainty and fear. It was all around us. It was almost like it beckoned us to join in—to release ourselves to that "not knowing what is to come," to take the counsel of our fears, to give up, to be afraid.

In this volume, I am going to be taking the opposite position.

I would have you knowing *precisely* what is to come; to *never* take the counsel of your fears; to *take heart*; to *find courage* in that wonderful Man, Jesus of Nazareth. And to do that, we'll be walking together through a series of Scriptures that

I call "Promises from the Mouth of God"—times when God Himself has given us His word.

But here's the backstory before we dive in.

On my birthday last year, I woke up very early, long before light, and got myself ready to do my typical run of the Cheyenne Cañon loop here in Colorado Springs. I do this two or three times a week, and I usually use the time I'm running to work through the Sermon on the Mount or a talk or, usually on Thursdays, to simply talk to *Him*. Well, my birthday last year was a Thursday—so, prayer. And as I was running up the slow climbing grade of the Cañon, silently going through my little litany, I began to realize the degree to which I was bored. Bored with the same prayer I so often prayed; bored with the reality that I was repeating things I so often say, and have so often said, to Him. And, in that moment—I was stopped now and looking up into the dark, starry sky—I was suddenly overcome with the knowledge of His *knowledge*. He already knew, already knows, everything I've ever done, thought, or said; already knows everything I'll ever do, think, or say. For me to ritualize my communications week by week, day by day with Him is like a subtle form of giving up. Such half-thinking intonations of prayer are for idols; I am trying to follow Jesus of Nazareth.

Well, that was the morning of my last birthday.

Now, fast-forward two-plus months. Also a Thursday morning.

I woke up that day thinking very particularly of my birthday realization and wanting to spend the time of *this* run in listening for His voice. So, as always, I got up, got ready, got my stuff together, and now I'm running the very same route in the very same darkness. And unless you're very much better at listening than I am, I was in that place where you're trying to block out all the swirling thoughts and worries and considerations that are attempting to crowd in. All the ups and downs of that particular week were trying to have their say to my conscious and unconscious mind; I was just running along, trying to keep them to the fringe.

And that was when I started, instead, to pray—to actively lay those worries and thoughts before Him, to *speak* them so I could get back to listening. And here's how I later wrote down what occurred shortly thereafter:

> And even as I started to ask for provision, it struck me: Yes, this prayer too He already knows. And has been working already to supernaturally answer. And that's when it hit me like the grandest realization: *I pray for things He's already promised.* And what a funny behavior! Instead of whispering, "Please provide for our family" for the millionth time, why not listen for one of His promises of provision and bring that to my heart and bring it right there before Him? He will provide; He's already promised. He will lead my steps; He's already promised. He will establish the course of my days within His will; He's already promised.

So, on that very morning, I began combing the Scriptures, collecting every single promise I could find that conformed to the necessities involved in that practice. I wasn't especially

15

interested in the many promises *ascribed* to God's perfect goodness; I wanted to hear the promises He'd spoken for *Himself.* Here's what I mean: throughout the psalms, for instance, David gives hundreds of wonderful promises of what he's sure the Lord has promised *him.* They are absolutely lovely to read—I am moved whenever I do—but those promises are not quite as absolutely given to *me*, are they?

What I've been after here are the promises, again, *straight from His mouth.* The unchangeable realities that are unchangeable *for all of us.*

You and me.

Everyone.

So, in these coming pages, I'm going to offer up one promise from His lips each day, with some accompanying thoughts He's given me around each. And FYI: I have put all sixty promises (thirty in this volume, thirty in the next) into an order that accounts for their relative importance—moving from the "highest-most-heavenly" down to the "still-important-but-functionally-most-earthly." I've prayed through the ordering of each section; I've taken each scripture from the translation that most powerfully brings it to light.

I'm ready to go…are *you?*

Shall we begin?

EUGENE LUNING
COLORADO SPRINGS, COLORADO
APRIL, 2020

Section One

ETERNAL LIFE

Promise
1

"For this is how God loved the world: He gave his one and only Son, so that everyone who believes in him will not perish but have eternal life. God sent his Son into the world not to judge the world, but to save the world through him."

John 3:16-17, NLT

First off, the all-important takeaway from this well-known promise: You, having believed in Jesus—having heard of Him, knowing of Him, knowing Him—*have* eternal life. Today, in Jesus, your present life, your future life, your endlessly continuing life is perpetual, unquenchable, and deathless in Him. Both life and death hold nothing that can haunt or daunt you. Your true life is found in Jesus now—the Son of the God of Heaven, the righteous Judge who came not to judge but to save.

What a wonderful place to begin our meditations.

Then, *get ready*—it's Greek time! Because most of us know the version of this verse that we memorized as little children, and we still intone the opening like this: "For God *so* loved the world." What we're doing there, consciously or not, is giving a quantitative understanding to God's love: "Oh yes, He loved us *so much.*"

That's not the way that John recorded Jesus' words.

The New Living Translation, the translation you read above, has it right: "For *this is how* God loved the world." The Greek word there is Οὕτως (*hoo-tohs*): "thus, in this way, like so, as follows." John has Jesus giving us a *qualitative* understanding.

Why do I care about you caring about this?

Because understanding the meaning of the *mechanics* of this promise both strengthens it and also spurs us into our own opportunity to respond. Take another read-through, now, of the meaningfulness of this way of understanding Jesus: "For *this is precisely the way* that God, once and for all time, loved the world: He gave the only Son He had so that anyone, everyone, people like you and me believing in Him would, from that moment, have no dealings with death; they would already be on to the endless life of Heaven. God once sent His Son, God has forever *already* sent His Son, not to judge the world but, through Himself, to set it free."

As you're sitting wherever you're sitting, as you're pacing or lying down or relaxing on your couch, you are already marked for endless life. There is nothing that sin, death or satan can do or say to change the equation of where you fit into this promise. You have already done the highest thing that human life can offer. You have met and given yourself to Jesus of Nazareth. Union with that wonderful Man from Galilee guarantees everything that is offered up in this glorious verse.

So, now free—what now?

I would say the power of properly understanding that Οὕτως from before is that, like Jesus, we can now find our *own* qualitative understanding of purpose. Here's what I mean: If God showed His love for the world "in this way"—Οὕτως—then we too are meant to love both God and the world "in this way."

So, if I may, here's how you and I—inheritors of this promise—should understand our lives *in light of this promise*: "For this is how you and I must love our God and all His children: we must give ourselves, our one and only life, so that everyone may have the chance to know Jesus, not perish, but have eternal life. God has now sent *us*, as the emissaries of His Son, not to judge the world but to point the world toward the Savior whose very life is salvation."

Do you see? This promise promises action—and purpose. And our template for engagement is today.

Let's go live the full reality of our Οὕτως—"in this way"—love for, and love from, Jesus.

Promise
2

"I solemnly assure you that the man who hears what I have to say and believes in the one who has sent me has eternal life."

JOHN 5:24, PNT

This, by the way, is not a carbon copy of yesterday's promise; otherwise Jesus wouldn't have spoken of salvation with such a different emphasis. In John 3, He was pointing to the Father's loving rescue plan through His life; here, He is pointing to His words and, by them, back at the Father. He is standing now in Jerusalem, just a day or two after healing the man at the Bethesda pool, and He is surrounded by crowds and also by enemies from among the religious leaders. And His purpose in the words directly before these words is that all people, then and now, will identify the works of the Father with the works of the Son.

So, let's talk about this promise, shall we? "I solemnly assure you that the man who hears what I have to say and believes in the one who has sent me *has* eternal life." Again, eternal life is the glorious promise. And, just like yesterday, it is yours—today. Whether you died this day or 10, 20, 40, or 80 years from now, the result is the same—you will dwell in, and with, Jesus forever. There is never any end to eternity's arc, because eternity has no arc; it isn't time, space, or linear experience. It's much better than that. It's the full love and full glory of Jesus. Full stop.

Now, having been reminded of the now-and-forever *promise* of this verse, what about the gateways through which Jesus says we walked to get there? If His words and our belief in the Father are prerequisites for eternal life, then they also must bear the requisite experiential qualities of eternal life *for today*. What I mean is: Rather than viewing His words and the Father as our gate-*keepers*, what if we, every day, thought of their presence in our lives as the experience of *already being inside*. Or, in other words: If we *have* eternal life, we are already in the Kingdom, so Jesus' words and His leading us to the Father are the new economy of our *experience* of our eternal life.

Listen to Jesus as He closes out the Sermon on the Mount: "Therefore, everyone who hears these words of mine *and acts upon them* may be compared to a wise man who built his house upon the rock. And the rain descended and the floods came and the winds blew and burst against that house and yet it *did not fall*" (see Matt. 7:24-25, paraphrased). You see, the words of Jesus of Nazareth are literally life; they are the direct exhalations of *the* Word of God who took on flesh. When we, every day, take something of His words and put them into practice, it's like we're aligning our flesh and its ways with *the* Way, *the* Spirit of Heaven. Actually, it's not just "like that." It actually *is* that!

Jesus is the "flawless expression of the nature of God" (Heb. 1:3 PNT), the perfect personification of both the Father and

Spirit's attributes within the perfect unity of the Godhead. Thus, when we take in Jesus' words, take on Jesus' meaning, *and then act upon them*, we are entering into deeper fellowship with the Father too—*and* the Spirit. We're practically, functionally dwelling in the midst of the Trinity.

So today, *having* eternal life, *having* heard and believed Jesus' words, *having* come into fellowship with the Father by the Son—will you *enjoy* the fruits of your eternal life by *hearing* and *living* Jesus' words and *entering more fully* into the Father's presence? Your experience of your eternal life can start today. It can start this very moment, right this second. You can have the fullest heavenly reality that's humanly possible—*right now!*—in giving your human life to Jesus' words and the Father's fellowship.

What an unbelievable opportunity is yours!

Your eternal life is now!

Promise
3

"Most assuredly, I say to you, he who believes in Me has everlasting life."

JOHN 6:47, NKJV

What a perfectly succinct promise for our hearts today. This is the third of our three "eternal (or everlasting) life" promises, and I'm maybe most moved by the simplicity and straightforwardness of this particular one. Jesus has only just finished feeding the 5,000 (maybe 8,000 or 10,000 with women and children) and He's presently speaking His way toward His famous "eat My flesh, drink My blood" teaching.

What I want you to do now is slow yourself down, take a deep breath, and open up that part of your mind that's ready to imagine. Because, yes, I want us to be there. To be alongside Jesus on the warm, windswept plain outside of Capernaum, looking down toward the sea, with the afternoon sun on both your faces.

He is looking into your eyes with particular affection. With anyone else, the intensity of this look would embarrass. But not with Him. Not from this Man.

"Most assuredly," He says—His eyes growing narrow and intense and filled with a fieriness of conviction. His shoulders are perfectly squared off in your direct direction, and now He reaches forward to rest both hands on the top of each of your shoulder blades. His hands are heavy and rough. You can feel their texture through the layers of your cloak and tunic.

"Most assuredly, *I* say to you." Jesus. This wonderful Man. *His* is the heart that is preparing to speak to *your* heart this glorious, timeless truth of your eternally interconnected destiny. Jesus. This dark, bearded Man from southwest Galilee. The One you've watched performing all those miracles of love, and of healing, and of power, and of light defeating darkness. The One whose words are *always* true, *always* good, *always* life.

"Most assuredly, *I* say to you, he who believes in Me." And He smiles as He speaks those words aloud. The man or woman or child—*you!*—the one who believes in the life and words and death and resurrection of Him—you are the one He's thinking of. All the weight of the promise He's about to promise is "most assuredly" only between His heart and yours, and you are the one with the belief He's about to reward. And how will He reward your belief in Him?

"Most assuredly, I say to you, he who believes in Me has everlasting life." *Has* it. Now. Right now. His whole face lights up as He leans a little closer with that smile and says, "You and me. Everlasting." Your life in Him was never meant for relegation to a single earthly life; that's not enough of you for Him. He would have you in His presence, within the intensity of this gaze, for a period of time that lasts past all time. He would have you taking walks together, talking of this or that, until the end of all the ages of ages. The intensity of His ardor for you is such that death couldn't kill it; it must last past this life to satisfy Jesus of Nazareth.

You will be with this Man forever.

Yours is a life and love that they'll write stories about.

His love for you is everlasting.

And now the life you possess is endless enough to match that love.

Section Two

"IT IS FINISHED"

Promise
4

"I assure you: Everyone who commits sin is a slave of sin. A slave does not remain in the household forever, but a son does remain forever. Therefore, if the Son sets you free, you really will be free."

JOHN 8:34-36, HCSB

Today, we're beginning another section of the promises that I've entitled "It Is Finished." These are the promises that tell us that our victory over sin, satan, death, and the grave is officially won, that the salvation work of Jesus is a *finished* work. There's nothing left for us to do but believe—and abide in Him.

The power of this first scripture, John 8:34-36, is in how Jesus couches the promise in three timeless statements of fact. Here they are:

- "Everyone who commits sin is a slave of sin." Fact.

- "A slave does not remain in the household forever." Fact.

- "A son does remain forever." Also a fact.

33

What the evil one, the world, the nature of sin doesn't want anyone to know is that the reality of sin is a *slavery to sin*. Our original fallen nature is like a prescription unto death that automatically proscribes any intimacy with the perfect, never-having-fallen, holy God of the universe. And, with that, sin is utterly cyclical. It turns in on itself; it draws its twisted form of "life" by perpetuating—reinforcing—itself. Thus, sin makes for its bearer a form of slavery, indenturedom—the inner life becomes the master of the man. That is Fact 1.

Now, Fact 2: "A slave does not remain in the household forever." In bondage as we *used to be* to sin, mastered by the realities of our likeness unto *Adam*, we were in the business of nothing more than slaving after our sinful nature's needs. We spent the bulk of our lives, *Pre-Jesus*, in either subtly or seriously going after the latest inclinations that happened to occur to our brokenness. Which is an untenable position. No life can live forever in slavery to its own corruption. So, no, we could *not*, in that state, remain forever in a household whose ways were built on another Kingdom's ways.

But, Fact 3: "A son does remain forever." The power of the promise Jesus is just about to make lies in the new identity He's pointing to in this last fact. *If* sin was slavery, *if* sin precluded eternal intimacy, then the only way to inherit the promise is to *inherit a new life*. A new identity. A new role in a different family altogether.

So, He says, you will no longer be out in the fields, fighting a futile fight against and yet *for* yourself; I will instead invite you into the Family. A son need never leave, He is saying, so how about I make you *into* a son, *into* a daughter of God?

How?

Well, here comes the promise:

"Therefore, if the Son sets you free, *you really will be free*." This wonderful older Brother, this One who co-existed in and with the Father in creating you, is the very One who'd draw you in. He is the One who arrived upon the earth for the express purpose of setting you free into a freedom that's really real in all its freeness. You are not "just a sinner saved by grace"—you are a *former* sinner graced with a freedom that's now inextricable from your new nature as a son or daughter of God. You are actually *done* with sin. You are *finished* with slaving unto yourself. Your Brother-in-Heaven has completed the work-on-earth that guarantees your forever-freedom and its ensuing sonship in the Kingdom of Heaven.

This is a fairly exciting promise to begin this section with, is it not?

Well, it's true. And it's yours.

Promise
5

"Come now, let's settle this,' says the Lord. 'Though your sins are like scarlet, I will make them as white as snow. Though they are red like crimson, I will make them as white as wool.'"

ISAIAH 1:18, NLT

Perhaps you remember the scene with Peter, having caught nothing all night while out fishing naked (the naked part is true, by the way—go look it up); do you remember when he catches sight of the Risen Jesus onshore and jumps in, swims in, and rushes up to see Him? It's in John 21. Can you picture that whole scene? How he, dripping wet, runs up the rocky shore and there Jesus is, tending a small fire with a few fish cooking on a spit? How Jesus motions toward the incoming boat, filled with the other disciples, filled with the fish He'd supernaturally helped them catch, and says, "Bring me some of those fish"? And how Peter, in the most classically Peter way, then sits on the gunwale of that boat and counts through every single fish, one by one? *"A hundred and fifty-three fish!"* he announces triumphantly.

"Come and have your breakfast, Peter," Jesus replies.

After which, walking along the shoreline, with the morning sun getting higher, Jesus does the business of reinstating Peter. You can almost hear the pebbly-crunchy sound of their sandals on the beach as Jesus, three times, reaffirms Peter's love—and His love for Peter. To me, the tone of that morning is, "Come now, let's settle this."

The reason this promise from the book of Isaiah is so striking to me is that 1) it's all the way back in the book of Isaiah, and 2) it sounds to me so much like Jesus. It's almost as if Isaiah himself, in the work of his office as prophet, had personally encountered the Son of Man *prior to His incarnation.* That matter-of-fact "Come now, let's settle this" and that description of our freedom from sin are simply *too much like Jesus.* We know that in Isaiah 6 the prophet has a direct encounter with God in the throne room of Heaven—fearsome and awesome. And I've been sitting here, pondering the wonderful possibility that, perhaps, he also got a sneak peek of our Savior Himself.

Anyhow, back to the promise.

Like Peter, I want you to imagine walking up out of the waters of the Sea of Galilee, with the wind-swell waves lapping at your feet. Ahead of you…is Jesus. He is sitting on a log, poking the fire with a long, sturdy stick, stirring the embers so that your breakfast gets cooked through. Looking up, He sees you and smiles. "Come now, let's settle this," He says to you.

But before you give Him a chance to properly settle your affairs, your sense of guilt and shame draws you back to a boat at the edge of the water. You turn your back on Jesus and walk on over and sit right down and begin counting—*enumerating*—all the ways you're not worthy. This is not a healthy confession; this is that thing you do whenever you're trying to (you think) "humble yourself" and "get right with Him."

Suddenly, He's standing right next to you. His eyes are not so pleased anymore.

"Come now, let's *settle* this," He says again. And He points back toward the fire and your breakfast, there.

As you sit yourself down across from Him, He's looking over the warmth of the fire and His eyes are gleaming with the same glowing as the embers. "Are you ready to listen to Me?" He asks.

You nod your head.

"Though your sins were like scarlet," He says, "I have *made* them as white as snow."

You try to interrupt Him. He waves you off.

"And though they were red like crimson," He continues, "I have made them white as wool; I have done all this, *forever*, at My Cross."

You have a great deal you'd like to say to Him—how you're fairly certain you're *still* such a sinner; that your theological understanding doesn't make room for such a complete wiping-away of sin—and yet it's difficult to argue with a Risen Jesus, isn't it?

He watches you across the fire.

Will you accept the reality of this promise?

Promise
6

"For I will be merciful to their unrighteousness, and their sins and their lawless deeds I will remember no more."

HEBREWS 8:12, NKJV

Two promises in one, really. That He will actively be merciful—full of mercy—to any and all acts and words and thoughts and patterns of unrighteousness that may crop up in and around you. That is the first promise.

The second: That your past, present, and future failings, lawless deeds, and willful or accidental recourses to your former nature will simply not be remembered anymore. They will "slip the mind" of God.

So before we go any further, can we stop to relish the *almost ridiculous lengths* He would go to to love us in our unloveliness? How, in the presence of our unrighteousness, our unrelenting fallen nature of sin, our brokenness, He draws *nearer*? How, seeing us needing mercy, watching us languish in our sinfulness, observing our shattering of Heaven's order, He came to set the whole thing right?

This is the heart of the One we follow.

And now let's talk about how He accomplished all He's promised here.

> *For I will be merciful to their unrighteousness, and their sins and their lawless deeds I will remember no more.*

But *how*, Jesus? *How* did You do this? To what degree is Your mercy and divine forgetfulness realistically available for people like us?

His friend, Paul of Tarsus, tells us in Colossians 2:13-14:

> *He has forgiven you **all** your sins: Christ has **utterly wiped out** the damning evidence of broken laws and commandments which **always** hung over our heads, and has **completely annulled** it by nailing it over his own head on the cross. And then, having drawn the sting of **all** the powers ranged against us, he exposed them, shattered, empty and defeated, in his **final** glorious triumphant act!* (PNT)

Were you catching the words I might've been trying to highlight?

Here they are:

- *All*
- *Utterly wiped out*
- *Always*
- *Completely annulled*
- *All*
- *Final*

And what were the words and phrases those descriptors were describing?

Read again:

- *All*—sins
- *Utterly wiped out*—the damning evidence of broken laws and commandments
- *Always*—hung over our heads
- *Completely annulled*—by nailing it over his own head on the cross
- *All*—the powers ranged against us
- *Final*—glorious triumphant act

The reason Jesus is so wonderfully full of mercy toward our unrighteousness is because Jesus doesn't believe we're unrighteous anymore. The reason He *just can't quite remember* all our sin and all our lawless deeds is because He hung them over His own head and *wiped them out*. And the book of the Law that the evil one would absolutely love to absolutely throw at us— it is finished. Completed. Over. In fact, the wondrous work of completion that was completed at the cross was also the final stand that satan could make against us. Now he is "shattered, empty and defeated" by the perfect Savior who is whole, full, and victorious.

Does it begin to make sense how pointless are our self-diminishing, self-destructive, self-abasing acts of old-fashioned religious-spirited contrition? We're always constantly beating ourselves up—forgetting to simply confess—and we act as if sin is the truest identity that most readily defines our lives and our way of life.

And all along, the *truest* thing is not us, or our sin, or our past; the *truest* thing is Jesus Himself. The One who is rich in mercy, almost humorously forgetful of our sin; who says, "That? Oh yeah, I'd almost forgotten that. Yes, I've already died for that, too."

That is the One who makes this promise today.

Is He the One you think you're following?

Promise
7

"But now, thus says the Lord, your Creator, O Jacob,
and He who formed you, O Israel, 'Do not fear, for
I have redeemed you; I have called you by name; you
are Mine!'"

ISAIAH 43:1, NASB

It is truly, deeply, *mightily* important that this promise of fearless redemption by the God who possesses us and knows our name is specifically spoken not just to Jacob—*as he was*—but to Israel—*as he is*—so that you and I can fully receive this promise. That probably sounded terribly confusing, I realize. So let's make sense of what the backstory to this promise is.

On a particular night in the course of human history, a man named Jacob—preparing to try to make peace with the brother he'd once cheated—is sleeping alone under the canopy of the stars. Suddenly, getting closer to daylight, he's awakened by a man. He probably doesn't know if the man is a bandit or some psychotic, and so he begins to fight and scrap and wrestle around in the half-darkness to overcome the intruder. All at once, a touch to his hip—it goes out of joint. Yet he will not release his hold over this other man. For at some point during the struggle, during this hours-long wrestle in the shifting from night to day, he has realized he's been struggling with God Himself. And now, rolling around in the dust and dirt, God says to him, "Let go of me. It is very nearly daylight."

And something rises up in Jacob's heart—a simple thought—and, from that grapple, he responds, "Not until you bless me."

"What is your name?" God asks him.

"I am Jacob," he answers.

"No longer," God replies. "You have now wrestled with men *and* God—and have won. That's why your name will now be Israel."

But something says to Jacob's, to *Israel's* heart that this is not enough; that the work of the night will not be completed without a full exchange. So he says, "Now tell me *Your* name."

And the Man, his God, responds: "Don't you know?"

And He blesses him before He departs.

> *But now, thus says the Lord, your Creator, O Jacob, and He who formed you, O Israel, "Do not fear, for I have redeemed you; I have called you by name; you are Mine!"* (NASB)

Today I would tell you that, for all the wonder and peace and eternal security of those words, I believe there are two ways to receive them. We can take them to heart and think of how nice and how lovely they sound in our ears; we might even memorize their cadence and tone for later consideration. I would call that the Jacob approach. It's the comfortable "Christian" way to receive promises in a sterile, safe, neutral sort of way. It is true, and right, and eminently a good thing.

I think there is far more for us in this verse.

If the highest height of the human experience is absolute conformity to the Way of Christ, then we *must* get a new name. We mustn't spend our whole lives striving and conniving and leaning back upon old promises like Jacob did before that night. We must be the new men and women. We must receive the *new* name Jesus actually has for us.

Consider the clauses of the promise, one by one.

"Fear not." Full stop. You are not permitted to be consumed with fear like you once were. The person who has struggled through the night in wrestling with Jesus has found His power to be *completely* able to overcome the day ahead. "Fear not." Stop fearing. Why?

"I have redeemed you." You have been bought. That's over now. There was a God who once created you, formed you, and, seeing you cut off by sin, came to redeem your life. He walked the earth and then interposed that very life for yours; He shed His blood so that you'd be free forever. Forever and ever. The price He paid was also the price of fear, sin, and death. So, "Fear not," He says, "for I have redeemed you."

"I have called you by name." A new name. A new identity. A new-creation lifeform. You and I are known, understood, wrestled-for and wrestled-*with* so that we'll know He knows our name. *Do you know He knows your name?* Have you had done with the old Jacob who'll always wonder? Have you looked into those eyes—from the position of intimate, even struggling embrace—and heard the way your name sounds from *those* lips?

For He says, listen to this, "you are Mine." You do not belong to anyone else. Even yourself. I have bought you with My blood and I value My blood highly: "you are Mine." You don't belong to any former Jacob-identity or self-evaluation or self-understanding: "you are Mine." The life that courses through you now is life that I have personally blessed by My Spirit: "you are Mine." Nothing that life or death or sin or satan can throw at you can harm you or hurt you: "you are Mine."

On the morning I'm recording these words, everything in the world would seem to say that all is descending into a great, maybe even terrible darkness. Fear is all around us. People feel untethered, unsure. They do not know what's coming and they feel afraid of the unknown—of the great not-knowing.

We have nothing to fear.

We have been redeemed—once for all time.

We are known, personally, by name.

We are His.

And along with Israel, by morning, we make bold to say, "Now tell me *Your* name."

And He replies, "Don't you know? I am Jesus."

Promise
8

*"I have swept away your sins like a cloud. I have scat-
tered your offenses like the morning mist. Oh, return
to me, for I have paid the price to set you free."*

Isaiah 44:22, NLT

This promise, with its triple reiteration of Jesus' victory over sin and its beautiful invitation to come and enjoy His love again, is our final promise in the "It Is Finished" section of these verses. And why did I put it in the last position?

Consider how it speaks to our hearts.

Have you ever felt, in the memory of your past sin or in the momentary experience of slipping back into those old ways, that it's almost like there's nothing around you *but* sin? Like the world itself is constructed of the stuff? That, in a very Romans 7 way, you *want* to do the right thing but the things you *tend* to do are the things you *don't* want to do? That each and every day is obscured, set off course, made terribly difficult by the lack of a clear view of what, precisely, to do?

Here's how Jesus receives that sense: "I have swept away your sins like a cloud." To Him, the persistent feeling we feel of envelopment by sin, of being surrounded, of powerlessness, of cloudy, foggy, overwhelming distraction—*is all a bit absurd!*

He has already swept all that away. They are like a cloud that He has (*phooooo!*) blown away.

But what about the real, and tangible, and destructive, and seemingly impossible-to-forget things we can't forgive ourselves for? What about our guilt and shame? Our nearly perfect memory for the mistakes we've made? What about how, at the one crucial moment, on that one particular day, we did that one unforgivable thing? The memory of it settles over our heart like a fog.

Listen to Jesus again: "I have scattered your offenses like the morning mist." That is how He views it. The past, to Him, *was* real, and tangible, and it had its destructive qualities, but it is terribly easy for Him to forget. Our guilt and shame He can lift like a weightless mist. Our nearly perfect memory for our mistakes is only exceeded by His faultless ability to forgive everything. Crucial moments, certain days, so-called unforgivable events are the reasons He came for us in the first place.

To do what?

He tells us: "I have paid the price to set you free." I have paid it. It is finished. And that price was for freedom. Not a religious understanding of what freedom might *mean*—no, for *freedom*. The ability to wake up every morning, put your feet on the floor, and live as freemen. The opportunity to work and to live and to love and to go to bed at night—as free men. "I have paid the price *to set you free.*" You are free *now*, so live that way. There is no reason to consider yourself enveloped by sin, surrounded by guilt and shame, when I've already done all the work to end those. You are wasting time when you do that. I have swept and scattered those away forever.

50

Which leaves us with my *absolutely favorite part* of this verse—the reason that I made it the last in this section. It's the personal, plaintive, intimate, leaning-toward-your-face way He makes His heart-to-heart invitation today and every day: *"Oh, return to Me."* Come back. Let's you and I be united once again. You had wandered into thinking of your sin, guilt, and shame again: *"Oh, return to Me."* You'd forgotten that the price I've already paid has already made you free: *"Oh, return to Me."* You'd accidentally glossed over the reality that you're My perfect child: *"Oh, return to Me."* You'd somehow started out your day without remembering that you're My favorite: *"Oh, return to Me."*

Friends, "It is finished." He has done it. All our sin and past is swallowed up in love.

Today, what the world needs to see is people *so truly free* that it calls all the rest of the world into question. Our lives are meant to be the contrast point. The light to the shadow.

Your life is the testimony of Jesus of Nazareth. And don't forget—you are free.

JESUS IS OUR SANCTIFICATION

Promise
9

"Moreover, I will give you a new heart and put a new spirit within you; and I will remove the heart of stone from your flesh and give you a heart of flesh. I will put My Spirit within you and cause you to walk in My statutes, and you will be careful to observe My ordinances."

EZEKIEL 36:26-27, NASB

Imagine meeting a Man on the street corner, or at a beach, or along a mountain path, and He immediately stops His day to talk with you, to hear your story, to know you. His initial opening question had caught your attention by its directness; you'd never met the Man before and now you're pondering and answering equally directly. For some reason, as you answer Him about your day and your life, you feel a strange relaxation of your usual guardedness. You are apt to trust this Man's ability to understand you. It is a strange sensation, instantaneously trusting Him.

Why, you ask yourself, *are you talking to this Man in this way?*

Perhaps it's because of the way that, when He first saw you, His eyes lit up. The look in His eyes was a look of immediate recognition—like He knew you. And then, too, there was the way He totally stopped His own momentum—His walk, His day—and became consumed with the answer you gave to His initial inquiry. And, especially, it was the way that, as you talked, He was so totally rapt with attention to every detail you felt so strangely comfortable sharing. Again, you had never met this Man till fifteen minutes ago; now, you're wanting to spend the rest of the day together.

What is it about this Man?

It feels to you like every ounce of His energy is brought into focus for the particular moment He's inhabiting. That's something. And the set of His eyes, the openness of His countenance seems to reflect an inner peacefulness that's nothing like anything in the whole world. He is fully alive, right now, to you. *Unto* you. *Directly toward* you. There is something within this Man that calls down into the inside of you and whispers of wonders and newness and new life offering itself to *you*. His presence, *even without words*, somehow speaks of a whole new thing He's offering, if you'll only just…

What is He asking? you wonder.

Whatever it is, you're interested in giving it.

Ezekiel 36 probably made absolutely no sense to Ezekiel's original hearers and readers because they'd never set eyes on Jesus of Nazareth. Ezekiel 36 should make *perfect* sense to us because we've already met, we already know, that Man I was just talking about.

I was describing, of course, Jesus Himself. As it's very clear He was, when you read through the four Gospels. His face and carriage and countenance and the way He spoke to any and all were the most arresting experience anyone had ever had. They found themselves "telling Him the whole story." They broke the necks of bottles of alabaster and anointed His feet. They sang in the streets when He came through. They clamored and clung to Him; they "jostled at His elbow."

Why?

Because the "new heart" and the "new spirit" of Heaven had been revealed, once for all time, and the people's "hearts of stone" and fleshly spirits yearned for exchange. Even if they couldn't have explained that fact. When they crowded Him by the tens and hundreds and thousands and tens of thousands, what they really wanted was Ezekiel 36. They wanted what was in Him, in them. And they had to be in that Presence as long as they had it.

The glory of this promise is that—*already and forever.* The realities it speaks of are *already and forever* yours. Jesus has *already and forever* given you a new heart and a new spirit; He has plucked the old right out of you. *Already and forever,* He has lavishly poured His own Spirit upon you and, to the degree you've desired, *within* you. There is every opportunity—now and *already and forever*—for you to knowingly walk in His statutes.

Jesus is your sanctification. He is the Way, the Truth, the Life.

And while I *love* the heavenly reality that everything I've just said is already and forever accomplished *for* you, I also appreciate the last line of this promise: "And you will be careful to observe My ordinances." There is demonstrable work for you to do, today. The only action that you properly bring to the equation of your sanctification is to get *lost* in the words and life of Jesus. To listen to Him. And obey.

So, let's go meet that Man in the circumstances of *this* day. It's the only one we have. And He's the only one we need.

Promise
10

"For I will pour water on him who is thirsty, and floods on the dry ground; I will pour My Spirit on your descendants, and My blessing on your offspring; they will spring up among the grass like willows by the watercourses."

Isaiah 44:3-4, NKJV

I appreciate how this promise takes into account that there are many layers to life, many aspects to our experience of existence. There are the basic daily needs. There are overall goals for meaning, for a purpose. There are the deeper spiritual needs of our inner life. There are the rich, nourishing possibilities of outward relationship, even possibly including having children—carrying on our line. And all of these, *all of them*, are directly included in the promise we are given today from the lips of the Lord. He knows exactly who we are—*what* we are—and His promises always extend to account for our whole being.

Remember, He *was* one of us. He knows us.

So let's look at how this promise is promised.

"For I will pour water on him who is thirsty." He sees your most basic needs. He sees your literal thirst for water, and He sees your inner need for refreshment every day of your inward life. He remembers when He hung upon the cross and said, Himself, "I am thirsty." There is not a single solitary experience of your humanity He's not familiar with. He wants you coming to Him with everything. "Jesus, I am thirsty. I am thirsty for Your presence. I am thirsty for enjoyment of Your Word." He is ready to pour water on all of that.

"And [to pour] floods on the dry ground." What a wonderful promise *that* is! In our quest to live a life of actual meaning amidst the absurdities, the seeming meaninglessness of the world around us, a certain feeling of dryness can begin to set in. All our greatest goals for our career—or our ministry, or our hopes and dreams—begin to seem like an endless, dry, sun-cracked field. Something that's lost its wonder. When, suddenly, in turning our eyes to Jesus, it's like a tidal wave of joy and peace and mercy rolls across the whole of it. Suddenly we're drenched, layers deep. Soaked in the glory of Jesus.

"I will pour My Spirit on your descendants." The first of our promises to deal in the next generation of belief. And whether or not you yourself are a parent or a grandparent, we *all* are involved in the great "generation-ization" that is the Gospel. The Way of the Kingdom of Heaven is the greatest, richest family tree in the history of humanity—its Head, its Father, is Jesus. The particular way it's wound and wended its way through the last two thousand years *has been family*— the Family of God. Whose lifeblood is the Holy Spirit *of* God. Who is the Spirit of Jesus Himself. "I will *pour* My Spirit on your descendants." And don't forget to ask for more for yourself!

"And [I will pour] My blessing on your offspring; they will spring up among the grass like willows by the watercourses." Isn't that a beautiful picture of promise? For all my friends and my family, for Jenny, for our children, I've been sitting here enjoying the image of blessing tumbling down. It rains down from Heaven upon my friends, my family, my Jenny, upon Hadley, Tripp, and Hoyt. The people He has blessed me with are sprouting up, springing up, taller than any of the grass of the fields. Their inner lives are watered with the Spirit of Jesus and waving like the beautiful willows that draw their life direct from a meandering river. That is what Jesus promises for me and mine. And for you and yours too.

> *For I will pour water on him who is thirsty, and floods on the dry ground; I will pour My Spirit on your descendants, and My blessing on your offspring; they will spring up among the grass like willows by the watercourses.*

Let us prove these promises today by our belief in them. Our most simple, basic trust. May we fall asleep tonight without thirst, drenched in Jesus, brimful of His Spirit, trusting our people's lives to His unfailing mercy.

For the One who promises is faithful and true. He is trustworthy and eminently to be trusted.

The One who makes these promises is Jesus.

61

Promise
11

"Then I will heal you of your faithlessness; my love will know no bounds, for my anger will be gone forever. I will be to Israel like a refreshing dew from heaven. Israel will blossom like the lily; it will send roots deep into the soil like the cedars in Lebanon. Its branches will spread out like beautiful olive trees, as fragrant as the cedars of Lebanon. My people will again live under my shade. They will flourish like grain and blossom like grapevines. They will be as fragrant as the wines of Lebanon."

HOSEA 14:4-7, NLT

Imagine a reality where your own human heart was perfectly faithful, where the utmost integrity of life and belief was your most natural reflex. Imagine a life where everything you ever touched was wondrously blessed, where you simply needed to focus your attention and—*yes!*—it blossomed. Imagine your everyday experience of life growing deeper, deeper, richer, richer, and, conversely, seeming to climb higher, higher, simply, beautifully. Imagine an existence where your own singular existence created sustenance for those around you, where the offshoot of your life was a fragrant grace. Imagine flourishing, fruitfulness, beauty.

I am talking about the exact life this promise offers you.

But first, let's consider every facet of who *He* is in this promise—how the life of our Lord makes possible everything we're destined to receive. Top to bottom, here you go; here's Him.

It is *He* who heals us of our faithlessness—that is *His* work—because His love is a love without any reasonable boundaries. His anger is already gone forever. It was poured out, once for all, at the Cross. And His presence in our lives is ever-constant; we are meant to experience it morning by morning like the arrival of the morning dew. He is the cultivator, the gardener who causes us to blossom and shoot roots and spread the branches of our life wide. *His* is the new, perfect DNA within our hearts that makes us stout and strong like the massive cedars of Lebanon. And yet His *too* is the shade under which we rest. No matter how tall and wide we grow, He's always greater, bigger, more massive. And it is in the restful shade of His loving presence that we'll learn to flourish and blossom and bring forth all the fruit of the vine.

Do you see how wildly interconnected is every single part of this promise—how our only possible way to experience it is while experiencing *Him*? He is the truth of this promise. *His* nature makes the possibilities of the promise possible. So a wise position—if you're interested in faithfulness, fruitfulness, rootedness, strength, and abundance—would be to consider the natural atmosphere of all these attributes. *Where* are they possible? *Where*, in fact, are they perfectly natural? *Where* might we wake up every morning and find these attributes springing from us, almost unconsciously, and experience the experience of this most blessed life?

Well, in the healing, loving, angerless, refreshing, constant, around-us, below-us, and above-us-ness that is Jesus. He has already proven every single adjective I just wrote—even the made-up ones!—by His overwhelmingly glorious earthly life. Jesus of Nazareth is no unknown quantity. If you read just one of the four Gospels, you already know everything you need to know.

But what we *don't* know—or maybe what we've only just begun scratching the surface of exploring—is what He's made possible *in us*. That is the mostly unknown quantity here. Just how far this thing can go. How truly, richly, *really* He has meant the things He said; how willing He is to meet our belief with an extraordinary, altogether superior experience of Heaven on earth. Something far more like we read of in the Book of Acts. Something wildly like the life of Jesus Himself.

Does that sound interesting to you?

Well, to me, too.

And so, just to remind you, it's all, only, today and forevermore to be found in deeper fellowship with Him. He is the source and the goal. The end and the means. Forever and ever.

Promise
12

*"I am the true vine, and My Father is the vinedresser.
Every branch in Me that does not bear fruit, He takes
away; and every branch that bears fruit, He prunes it
so that it may bear more fruit. You are already clean
because of the word which I have spoken to you. Abide
in Me, and I in you. As the branch cannot bear fruit
of itself unless it abides in the vine, so neither can you
unless you abide in Me. I am the vine, you are the
branches; he who abides in Me and I in him, he bears
much fruit, for apart from Me you can do nothing. If
anyone does not abide in Me, he is thrown away as a
branch and dries up; and they gather them, and cast
them into the fire and they are burned. If you abide
in Me, and My words abide in you, ask whatever you
wish, and it will be done for you. My Father is glorified by this, that you bear much fruit, and so prove
to be My disciples. Just as the Father has loved Me, I
have also loved you; abide in My love."*

JOHN 15:1-9, NASB

If you know me even passingly, then you know this is my
favorite set of verses, something like a "life section" that I'll

never stop talking about. Why? Because show me another place where Jesus so explicitly states: "This is the whole purpose of life; this is how you do life in the proper heavenly way." And what is the key word that unlocks this whole set of verses? "Abide"—*eight times in these nine verses*! And what a marvelous, mysterious word it is. To have Jesus say, "Do this one thing," and then to get to spend the rest of our lives learning to do it? What could be better!

So, over the years, I've tried many times, in many ways, to teach through this passage, and today I'm going to try something different with you.

Can you and I agree that Jesus Himself is life, that both the bestowal of life and also the proper conduct of life both find their fulfillment in Him? Or, to say it more simply: Isn't Jesus the way to eternal life and *also*, by following in His earthly footsteps, the highest and best way to live?

Okay, so looking at these verses and agreeing that Jesus is life, how about we substitute some of their mystery for the simplicity of *just*-Jesus? Because if "abiding" is the act of living in and attaching one's life to *the* Life, then let's strip these verses down to their simplest possible version.

Take a read and we'll see if it works:

> "I am the true life, and My Father is the creator and tender of that life. Every person who labels himself with My life and yet doesn't look anything like Me, My Father takes away; and yet the one whose life looks even a little like Mine, He works on so that he looks even *more* like Me.

You are already totally set free in the direction of living My life because of My words that you have already taken to heart. Live your life inside My life, like My life, and you will find that I'm living My life inside of you, remaking you. As disconnected things cannot possibly share the same vital life, so neither can you share My life unless you're connected to Me. I am life, you need life; the one who lives in Me and attaches his whole life to My life, and I to his, he will look like Me and bear My stamp. But apart from Me you will always be lifeless.

"If anyone does not live his life in My life and attach himself to Me, he has made a conscious choice—for disconnection and a false version of life. He will find himself eventually gathered—*forever*—into a complete experience of such disconnection and falsity and non-life.

"But if you live your life in My life and attach yourself to Me, and My words live inside you and attach themselves to your heart, go ahead: ask absolutely anything in my name—anything you wish, anything you hear *true* life calling for—and it will be done for you. My Father is glorified by this, that your life looks like Mine, just like Mine, and so you prove to be disciples of My life. Just as the Father has loved Me—the embodiment of life itself—so I have also loved you; live your

life in My life and attach yourself to My life and
My love."

The promises of these most wonderful words of
Jesus can be listed, as such:

- Guaranteed fruitfulness

- Being made holy

- Direct transfusion of true life, life to life

- Real heavenly purpose

- Answered prayer

- Interconnected enmeshment in the Godhead

- Bringing the Father glory

- Being truly known as Jesus' disciple

- Being loved by Him and invited deeper into
  His love

And so I apologize to the many of you who hear me
speaking enough that you already know what's coming, but
sorry—here it comes again.

The key to receiving all of the blessing of these promises,
the linchpin for living your life in His life and proper attach-
ment unto Jesus is—*abiding*.

To abide in Him.

There is nothing higher or better for your human life. You
and I must abide in Jesus.

And if you're continuing to wonder what that marvelous,
mysterious word might mean for you, go back again to the
idea of life. *Whose* life are you endeavoring to live? Your life

alone, or His life *together*? Are you waking up today still under the impression that your life is the "chief end" of you, or are you starting to realize that life is *that Man*? That wonderful bearded man from Nazareth in Galilee.

May you and I abide in Him and He in us today. Amen and amen.

Section Four

THE HOLY SPIRIT

Promise
13

"Suppose you went to a friend's house at midnight, wanting to borrow three loaves of bread. You say to him, 'A friend of mine has just arrived for a visit, and I have nothing for him to eat.' And suppose he calls out from his bedroom, 'Don't bother me. The door is locked for the night, and my family and I are all in bed. I can't help you.' But I tell you this—though he won't do it for friendship's sake, if you keep knocking long enough, he will get up and give you whatever you need because of your shameless persistence. And so I tell you, keep on asking, and you will receive what you ask for. Keep on seeking, and you will find. Keep on knocking, and the door will be opened to you. For everyone who asks, receives. Everyone who seeks, finds. And to everyone who knocks, the door will be opened. You fathers—if your children ask for a fish, do you give them a snake instead? Or if they ask for an egg, do you give them a scorpion? Of course not! So if you sinful people know how to give good gifts to your children, how much more will your heavenly Father give the Holy Spirit to those who ask him."

LUKE 11:5-13, NLT

So, suppose instead you went to the house of your friend, Jesus—whether at midnight or whenever—wanting to borrow a dash of His Holy Spirit. You say to Him, "The whole world is in need of Your presence, a fresh experience of Your visitation, and I myself have nothing to give them." And instead of, say, calling out from His bedroom, you can hear Him rushing to the door; it gets thrown open and almost pulls you in with its gust of wind blowing by. "I'm so glad you called on Me *first*," Jesus smiles. "My door is *never* locked, and I'm absolutely never in bed. I can help any time, any minute, any day."

Furthermore, Jesus tells us this Himself—that what He does He does for friendship's sake—*you are His friend*—and if you continually knock, He will continually answer because of your joyous persistence. And it is He Himself who tells you *keep on asking*, and you will literally receive what you actually ask for. He says *keep on seeking*, and you will find. Keep on knocking, and the door of the Kingdom will be opened to you. For everyone who asks—"everyone" most certainly including you—receives. Everyone who seeks—"everyone" still most certainly including you—finds. And to everyone who knocks—and you are still a part of "everyone" here—the door will be opened.

If you yourself are a father—or if you can imagine a *good* father—if his children ask for a fish, he would not give them a snake, would he? Or if they ask him for an egg, would he give them a scorpion?

"Of course not!" Jesus laughs as He says.

"So if sinful people know how to give good gifts to their children," and here Jesus grins with the readiness of a wonderful reminder coming, "or, if *formerly* sinful people whom I've set free with My blood know how, then *how much more*—listen— how much more will your heavenly Father give *the Holy Spirit* to those who ask Him!"

Today, as we move into a new section of promises about the gift and arrival of the Holy Spirit, I could think of nothing more important for us than particularizing those verses for our New Covenant context. When Jesus first spoke those words back in Luke, He was standing surrounded by His twelve best friends—twelve best friends who *hadn't* seen the Cross, Resurrection, Ascension, or Pentecost. Those men *were in the dark*. Even though they were standing with Jesus, they lacked nearly everything we possess. And even though I'd certainly give my right arm for just ten minutes of walking with Jesus around Galilee, it's important we remember: *We are in a privileged position.* We have been given the knowledge of Jesus, the Cross, and Resurrection *already accomplished*, and the power of the Ascension and Pentecost *ours for the taking*. Do you know how much it cost the Twelve to get to just where you are?

I'll help you: *Everything.* Their careers, their normalcy, their family life, the idea of their natural future. All of it.

So, back to this promise.

The reason that I went back through and put Jesus' midnight parable into its positive present new-covenant paradigm is because, if the presence and experience of the Holy Spirit is *absolutely everything* for followers of the Way of Jesus, then we've *already got everything we need*. Or at least, the *promise* of everything we need. If you can go to Jesus morning, noon, or night and knock, ask, and seek for *absolutely anything you desire*, then what do you *actually* desire? Do you go to Him with the cares of the present day, the hopes for a better tomorrow, the dreams you cherish for a certain picture of the future you've imagined? (And all of those prayers are fine, by the way!)

But will you also stop to remember that *the very life of Heaven*—the Holy Spirit—has been offered to you *with no limit*? If you, being formerly of the sinful race of Adam, know how to give a good gift to a child, how much more—*how much more!*—will the heavenly Father give His Spirit to the brothers and sisters of *Jesus*?

You are already in the House; why not ask for more?

Why not ask, as long as you're already inside the door, already being led past the foyer into the kitchen, already expected to ask for the everything that's already yours—why not ask for all the power in the whole universe? Why not ask for the life source, the engine, the inner engineering, of the inner life of Jesus Himself?

That is the reality of the Holy Spirit of God. He is the *Holy. Spirit. Of God.* He is the One who spoke to, empowered, manifested in, and showed the reality of who was Jesus. The words and actions and miracles and manifestations of glory that we see throughout the four Gospels were the works of the Holy Spirit—*in Jesus.* The words and actions and miracles and manifestations of glory that we see in the Book of Acts were the works of the Holy Spirit—*in fools and idiots just like us!*

So, here's my question for you today: Will you come and knock, ask, seek, *and then get* what's properly meant to be yours? Will you take Jesus at His word and then ask for and receive more of the Holy Spirit's presence in you *today*? Will you move beyond your clean, clear, theologically fascinating (I'm sure!) perspective on the Holy Spirit and get *engulfed* by that Holy Spirit?

The Church today—the Body today—is perfectly fine if you're interested in things that are perfectly fine.

I'm not.

I'm interested in seeing the four Gospels happening in *you*. I'm interested in seeing the Book of Acts happening *again*. And the only path available for men and women who share that experiential interest is to follow the Way of Jesus by the indwelling of the Holy Spirit.

Who, by the way, has already been promised to you.

By Jesus.

Right here.

Put it this way: Imagine there's a dinner bell ringing in the doorway of Heaven, right this minute: *"Come and get it!"*

Well, I'm telling you there is.

Will you come and get it?

Promise
14

"And I will pray the Father, and He will give you
another Helper, that He may abide with you for-
ever—the Spirit of truth, whom the world cannot
receive, because it neither sees Him nor knows Him;
but you know Him, for He dwells with you and will
be in you. I will not leave you orphans; I will come to
you."

JOHN 14:16-18, NKJV

The reason I find this particular promise to be particularly potent is because of how it stacks upon itself—promise
after promise, each contingent upon the other—almost like
a Russian nesting doll. And yet that final phrase, that last
clause at the end of verse 18, may be one of the least celebrated,
least appropriated realities of the Holy Spirit in the life of the
Church. But we'll get to that in a minute or two.

First, the outer promise—the biggest, most obvious of
the nesting-doll truths offered up here: "And I will pray the
Father." I (meaning Jesus) will ask the Father for you. Do you
understand—*can* you understand—the almost-too-wonderful
scene that is constantly playing out in the Throne room of
Heaven? The fact that Jesus of Nazareth, that wonderful Man
who ascended to Heaven *as a man*, is constantly interceding

with the Father on your behalf? That He casually leans on the shoulder of the Father and speaks of *you* to Him; that He's persistently making the Father aware of His delight in you, His pleasure in you, His saving of you?

"And I will pray the Father, and He will give you another Helper"—the Holy Spirit, who is the highest gift of Heaven. The portion of the Holy Spirit that you have personally received has been bestowed on you by express decision of the Father and Son. They have, together, made a choice that you are, without a doubt, one of theirs and, for that reason, a proper bearer of the life of Heaven within. The Helper, the Holy Spirit, is meant to intimately interconnect you *between* the Father and Son as part of their personal intimacy.

An overwhelming thought, that one!

"That He may abide with you forever." Forever. Abide with you forever. Not to cut and run whenever you make a mistake or don't have the answers. No, He abides with you forever. Today. Tomorrow. Forever. And He is meant to consistently overtake more and more of your inner life—*as you'll let Him*—so that your spirit becomes more *Holy* Spirit.

"The Spirit of truth, whom the world cannot receive, because it neither sees Him nor knows Him." His work, invisible, is truth. He arrived at Pentecost for the strengthening and empowerment of the inner lives of those individuals—*why?* So that they might, by their witness and lives and lifestyle, point to the One who is the Truth, *is* the Way, *is* the Life. The world hasn't always been ready to receive that truth. But the Spirit in us always continues to point to *Him*.

"But you know Him, for He dwells with you and will be in you." My friend, read those words again: *"in you."* The very Spirit of God, the life of Heaven, the inner interconnection between the Father and Son: *"in you."* The answer to your every self-doubting, serial questioning of your salvation status: *"in you."* The One to whom Jesus Himself would stop to question, ponder upon His actions, and then, in power, make the exact choice of Heaven: *"in you."*

And then comes that final clause I mentioned before.

"I—*Jesus*—will not leave you as orphans; *I will come to you.*" I—again, *Jesus*—will come to you. Not *just* My Holy Spirit, not just a friendly visitation of part of the Godhead. No, *I* will come to you. The bodily, bearded Man from Galilee; the One the disciples would immediately readily recognize; the Savior who died and then rose again. *He* will come to them—*and to us*!

What are we to make of this final, wonderful promise? What does it mean in the context of the Holy Spirit's presence and work?

Well, the apostle Paul himself not only hinted at what I'm about to write, he very explicitly *wrote* what I'm about to write. Read it in Colossians 1:26-27: "[You] are those to whom God has planned to give a vision of the full wonder and splendour of his secret plan for the sons of men. And the secret is simply this: Christ in you! Yes, Christ *in you* bringing with him the hope of all glorious things to come" (PNT).

My friend, the greatest work of the Holy Spirit—and something you almost never hear mentioned anywhere—is that He literally translates the physical, fleshy, real, risen Jesus so that

He's able to live His own life inside *your* life. The Holy Spirit doesn't just bring the Holy Spirit to live in you. The Holy Spirit brings Jesus—*that Man*! That wonderful, glorious, righteous, funny, amazing Man we've learned to love has come riding the coattails of His own Spirit into *your* spirit! When you talk to Him, you are not just talking to the distant reality of His presence in the Throne room of Heaven; as far as *you* know, the Throne room of Heaven *is within you*! Because, again, "*Christ* in you, the hope of glory" (NKJV)!

> *And I will pray the Father, and He will give you another Helper, that He may abide with you forever—the Spirit of truth, whom the world cannot receive, because it neither sees Him nor knows Him; but you know Him, for He dwells with you and will be in you. I will not leave you orphans; I will come to you.*

Does it get any better than this series of promises, all nested within each other, one after another?

My answer would be—no!

Promise
15

"But the Helper, the Holy Spirit, whom the Father will send in my name, he will teach you all things and bring to your remembrance all that I have said to you."

JOHN 14:26, ESV

I remember the exact day when I actually began to believe this promise. I was standing on the upper deck, the leader-meeting deck, facing a group of staff and leaders up at Young Life's Malibu Club in British Columbia. If you've ever been there, you know exactly where I'm talking about. (If you haven't, you probably need to Google the whole place for pictures.) Standing there, with the warm sun on my face, with the breeze blowing down the inlet and over all of us, I was talking to the leaders about that night's cabin-time—"cabin-time" being that time after the hearing of the Gospel when leaders and kids go back to their cabin to talk and discuss. Essentially the whole reason that every Young Life leader in the whole world—domestic and international—even gets kids to go to camp. The half-hour or hour when everything often changes in kids' hearts. In some ways, the whole heart of Young Life itself.

Anyhow, I was talking about the questions I might myself use to get kids talking that evening—simple openers that might get them going and more comfortable sharing. And I don't quite remember if a leader specifically asked or if it was the Holy Spirit Himself in my heart that prompted, but all at once I felt all stirred with a *complete* realization. A word from the Lord for me—and for those leaders.

I said something like: "Listen, there's every possibility that one of your kids is going to ask a question tonight while you're in there that you absolutely don't have an answer to. And I've always said to leaders, just be honest—say you don't know; it's good for your kids to admit that you don't have all the answers.

"Well, I'm telling you tonight, by the exact words of Jesus, that even if you don't have the answer to that question *the Holy Spirit inside you does.* It has been promised us that when we stand before governors or kings—or a bunch of teenage kids— it will be *given* us what to speak. And that He will teach us all things and bring remembrance of what Jesus said.

"So tonight, if you sense you're getting *that* question from a kid—where you already know you don't know the answer— I'm asking you to slow down, to pray, and to *ask for the answer.* The Holy Spirit within you already knows. And He's been sent to live inside you, straight from Jesus, and part of His purpose is tonight with these kids—for that question. Let's all get a little wild in making Him our first recourse."

I could literally watch the way those leaders took courage. How they sat up in their chairs and faced that camp-worth of kids with belief. And I'll never forget the remainder of that camp week, hearing the stories of *how it worked*, how the Holy

Spirit *spoke*. How, seemingly out of the blue, leaders felt armed with a whole new set of answers, knowledges, lines of new questions—*by Him.*

Nothing is any different for your day today. This promise has been promised to you for your everyday life. The Holy Spirit, sent by Jesus and the Father, has been bestowed on you in order that you'd never lack knowledge, or His words, in any situation. So in *any* situation, sensing you lack knowledge or access to His words, your very next impulse and thought and action is approaching Him. "Holy Spirit, because You came to me from Jesus, because You've been sent to me by the Father, please tell me *exactly* what I need to know here. Please reveal. Please speak."

What an unbelievably *believable, actionable* promise! And what an opportunity to believe, act, and experience.

All the wisdom and insight and knowledge and brilliance that could ever inhabit the entirety of the universe is stored up in the Mind of the God who created it all. And the literal Spirit of that God now lives in you. And the Son of God has said: "Ask *and receive.*"

And there is nothing *not* included in the promise of being personally taught "all things." *All things are on the table for you!* And there is never *not* a moment when, needing a word from Jesus, needing some insight into His mind and teachings, *you can't simply ask.*

He has promised.

He has promised *you.*

The wondrous power and mind of the Holy Spirit are yours. They are, right now, *within* you.

Promise
16

"But you are to be given power when the Holy Spirit has come to you. You will be witnesses to me, not only in Jerusalem, not only throughout Judea, not only in Samaria, but to the very ends of the earth!"

ACTS 1:8, PNT

Imagine traveling in a totally foreign country where the language and most of the cultural customs are utterly different from your own. Each morning as you rise and enter the heart of the capital city, it's more of the same—that feeling of confusion, disconnectedness, strangeness, feeling out of place. Every single street you enter, every marketplace you wander, you are surrounded by the sound of a tongue not your own. To you, even though there's a sort of beauty in this language you cannot understand, it also presents a barrier to any form of intimacy, invitation, belonging. The lack of clear understanding hampers any plans for staying. You're beginning to dream of going home. When...

What's that? What's that sound you're hearing?

It's coming across the top of the roofs from the next town square over.

Inclining your ear, you begin to walk through the narrow, shadowy street that connects your street with that next open-air plaza. The closer you get, the more you begin to realize that the strangeness of that sound is actually found in its *familiarity*. Arriving, you realize what it is.

Someone is actually speaking your native tongue.

It's the very first time you've heard another voice speaking your language since the day you arrived to the city. Your heart rises with the joy of home. You begin to listen to what the speaker above is saying:

"O Jesus," he says, "You are so good, *so* kind, *so* great and powerful in the lavishing of Your love for us. You are my God and my friend, Jesus. I love You. I delight to have Your Spirit within. I delight that You have come and set us free from sin and death. I delight in Your Cross and Resurrection. O Jesus, I am Yours—forever and ever. Jesus, I am Yours."

Ten days before this day, the man who stands above you speaking these words in your native tongue was actually standing with that Man, Jesus. And that Man, Jesus—the one this speaker calls his God—said to him these words: *"But you are to be given power when the Holy Spirit has come to you. You will be witnesses to me, not only in Jerusalem, not only throughout Judea, not only in Samaria, but to the very ends of the earth!"*

Now *you*, a person from the very ends of the earth standing in the Jerusalem sunshine, are hearing the witness. You had never heard of Jesus until this moment. You weren't here to hear His messages, to see His miracles. But the odd experience of hearing the language of home, of seeing the look in the man's eyes above you, is an experience of a heavenly power.

Whatever possesses the inner life of this strange speaker—or, perhaps, *Whoever* possesses his spirit—is Someone you'd be interested to know of. With the rest of the crowd, you press closer to hear. By the end of this day, you'll be baptized into the Name.

My friend, isn't it a wonderfully wondrous thought that the Spirit of Pentecost is the very same Spirit that dwells in us, today? That the power Jesus promised to His friends on the day of the Ascension is the same power He's given us? That there is nothing in the whole world that can stop the Holy Spirit from proclaiming the name of Jesus of Nazareth to the whole world? That the battle plan for the Kingdom of Heaven's advance across the face of the earth is nested within your heart and mind?

With that, some questions for you today:

Do you believe that's true?

Do you believe the Spirit of Jesus is within you?

Are you willing, during this day, to actually listen and be obedient to His still, small voice?

Will you start to let the operation of some of this day, part of this day, all of this day be left up to His leading?

If you opened up your mouth to speak of Jesus *and found you were speaking in a foreign tongue*, would you keep going?

In fact, how far are you willing to go?

To the street corner?

To the very ends of the earth?

Well, the only way to chase this promise, to enjoy its fruit, to *arrive* to the ends of earth is to allow the Holy Spirit access to the very ends of yourself.

That might be the highest purpose for this particular day.

Let's go see how far this goes.

Promise
17

"When the Spirit of truth comes, he will guide you into all truth. He will not speak on his own but will tell you what he has heard. He will tell you about the future."

JOHN 16:13, NLT

Despite the absolute indivisibility of the Father and Son—the complete lack of distance between their interconnectedness—let's imagine, for a moment, that such a space existed. There they are, inhabiting the very same Throne amidst the celestial glories of the Throne room of Heaven (see Rev. 3:21). And yet, let's imagine they're about six inches apart from rubbing shoulders. Even though we're perfectly aware that Jesus only ever did things that He'd already seen His Father doing, even though the Godhead is a perfect unity—what if there was the *tiniest* gap between them? And what if—during the act of Creation, during the time of Jesus' life upon earth, right now on the Throne of Heaven—they had to talk across that distance?

Then I'll tell you right now—that distance is the Holy Spirit.

The Holy Spirit is not only the inner life of Jesus while He walked the earth and did the will of the Father; not only

93

the actual Spirit that *is* the interconnectedness of Father, Son, and, yes, Spirit; the Holy Spirit is also the very atmosphere of Heaven itself. He is that possible, potential area between the Father and Son's shoulders. He is the heavenly wavelength across whom their conversations happen. He is the mutual thought they think and think, "Hey, *I* was just thinking that!" When they hatch together a plan for something big—say, like the six days over which they created Creation—they are communicating both with and through the Holy Spirit.

The Holy Spirit is the relationship of the Godhead.

And *precisely* when that Spirit of truth comes from the Father and the Son, He will guide *you* into all the truth that the Father and Son possess—that is, every truth that's ever going to be possibly possible to ever possibly know in the whole possibility of time and space! You and I are meant to take this promise and immediately put it into practice; we are meant to be searchers and seekers and, more importantly, *listeners* after "all the truth." For where does the Holy Spirit *get* all this truth?

"He will not speak on his own but will tell you *what He has heard*." What He has *heard*! What has been leaned across that infinitesimal space between Father and Son—their perfectly indivisible and yet separately personified relational unity—and breathily spoken: *the Holy Spirit hears all that!* He hears the latest plots and schemes and willings and inner workings of the Father and Son, and we are literally encouraged to ask what the Father and Son are thinking of!

I'll put it to you this way: What are you more interested in hearing today—the clanking, clunky thoughts you *think* you're having (in reality, mostly just your unconscious, reactionary experience toward rapidly changing visual stimuli), *or* the thoughts of Jesus and the Father? Two different channels; which do you choose?

And I'll even make the choice more obvious for you.

"He, *the Holy Spirit*, will tell you about the future"—what is to come—the Holy Spirit will soothsay! He will speak to you of, lead your readings in the Word to prepare you for, He will wash across the landscape of your inner life to set your heart ready for the coming of the next things. The Holy Spirit already knows what's coming. He is the Spirit and mind of God *within you!*

My friend, if you're interested in the truth, in the inner workings of the relationship of Jesus and the Father, in the future—*then you're in the right place.* Or, actually, *the Holy Spirit is in the right place.* (And, in case you haven't been paying attention at all, that place *is you!)*

You are the particular place in the world where He's chosen to land. *You* are the one where Heaven's life is happening today. *You* are a receiver of the truth, love, and future God knows. *You* are a Holy Spirit-rich person.

Do you want more of Him?

Great!

Simply ask of Jesus and the Father—it will be granted.

Do you want to *experience* all of this more?

Great!

Today is the day when you may do that. The opportunity's all yours.

Promise
18

"My sheep hear My voice, and I know them, and they follow Me; and I give eternal life to them, and they will never perish; and no one will snatch them out of My hand. My Father, who has given them to Me, is greater than all; and no one is able to snatch them out of the Father's hand."

JOHN 10:27-29, NASB

I have to tell you, I'm very excited about this promise and what we're going to do with it. So first, a little unpacking—*then the fun!*

This promise is specifically for and about the flock of sheep who belong to Jesus, who is the Good Shepherd, and the Gate for the sheep—*and we are those sheep.* The absolute indestructibility of the power of the initial promise here ("My sheep hear My voice") is, now and forever, underwritten by the rest of these words. In fact, take them from back to the front to see how guaranteed is your position in Him.

"No one is able to snatch them out of the Father's hand." That's where you live—in the hollow of the Father's hand. The blood of Jesus has eternally purchased you, and He has handed you off to His Father, holy and blameless, and your life and spirit rest in the Father's palm. *And nothing can change that fact!*

For, "My Father, who has given them to Me, is greater than all." The Father, who is greater than all, has given us back to Jesus. Our salvation was a one-time act that handed our lives from satan unto Jesus, who then turned around and gave us to His Father. Our *sanctification* is a wondrous lifetime experience in which the Father, handing us back to Jesus, watches us grow and learn and become like Him. We are servants within the hand of Jesus now.

"And no one will snatch them out of My hand." That's Jesus' final word on the "Can you lose your salvation?" question. Once you've given your heart and soul and mind to Jesus, you are *always* His; there is no earthly or hellish power that can claw you back.

For, "I give eternal life to them, and they will never perish." Our High Priest—to paraphrase Hebrews 7:16—receives His ministry *not* by virtue of any outward command, but by "the power of an indestructible life within." That is the life He possesses—and that He gives. Indestructible. Imperishable. Now ours.

"And they follow Me"—yes, we will, Jesus!

"And I know them"—oh, thank You, Jesus!

And, *"My sheep hear My voice."* Us. You and me. We. Today. I may hear His voice. You may hear His voice. You and I together may hear His voice.

So let's not spend our time in talking about or reading about the reality of hearing His voice; *let's hear His voice!* Let's use the rest of the next few minutes you'd planned to read my words in listening for His words. *Let's experience this promise being true!*

From my own experience, His voice can come in unexpected thoughts about a verse He brings to mind, in pictures that seem to appear to you, or in totally original things He impresses upon you.

And the last-last thing I'll say: If you're thinking right now, "This is a crazy thing to ask of us," I'd remind you—the only crazy thing is how often we *aren't doing this!* The promise stated before is the actual promise of God; our best and only response is *what we're going to do right now.* So let's actually, properly respond—by listening.

Your Personal Time of Silence

Notes below on what He spoke to you:

_____

_____

_____

_____

_____

_____

_____

_____

_____

_____

Promise
19

"And your ears shall hear a word behind you, saying, 'This is the way, walk in it,' when you turn to the right or when you turn to the left."

ISAIAH 30:21, ESV

When you think of the worldwide Body of Christ—*the Church*—generally you immediately begin thinking of *the churches* on the street corners around your town. And even as you just read those words—"the churches"—I can almost guarantee your mind conjured up this, that, or the other brick-and-mortar church somewhere nearby you. At some point in the history of that "church," men and women came together, voted to incorporate, voted upon leadership, picked a name, raised money, built. Of course, they prayed their ways through those processes, sought the Lord, encouraged each other, felt the push and pull of the Spirit, but at heart, most or all of them had somewhat similar startup stories.

Now, at a location—there's a "church."

Each Sunday, at a particular time, there are "services."

And the original vision may or may not be the overriding purpose of the people standing, sitting, or kneeling in those services in that building. And for that reason, whether that church was started five or five hundred years ago, I want us to consider the above promise from the other, more grassroots perspective.

Because, when you think of the worldwide Body of Christ—*the Church*—what you should really think of is what Jesus said in Matthew 18:20: "For where two or three gather in my name, there am I with them" (NIV). For even as you read those words, "two or three" and "I am with them," you are getting your best description of the definition of the *actual* Body of Christ—the literal Body *of Christ*, Jesus Himself, translated into our presence by the Holy Spirit—meeting directly with a handful (or houseful...or megachurchful) of His disciples. At any point in the history of the world since Pentecost, men and women may come together, experience His presence, receive His leadership, bear His name, obtain His provision, and be built up by Him. Of course, on occasion we've forgotten about the first-handedness of this arrangement and been carried away by process, system, committee, building campaigns, lighting, smoke machines, good tech, etc.

But now, at any location, we may re-comprise the Body.

Sunday or not, at any time, there's possibility of the Presence.

Which—with all that as a prelude to the words of today's promise—finally brings us to the words of today's promise.

If it only takes "two or three" to step into the inner sanctum of a living, Churchly fellowship with Jesus, then you're presently 50 percent or, at worst, 33.3 percent of the answer to everything the world needs in order to experience Him. Do you believe that? Does the simplicity of that math excite you? Or daunt you?

And if, at every single twisting and turning of the day's ways, you've been promised direct, personal, whispering-in-your-ear directives of the *true* Way, are you availing yourself of that wonderful promise? Do you listen? Is your ear open?

Because whether you're turning to the right or left today, whether you're on your way to church or work or workout, you are a miraculous component of a miraculous composite that is Jesus Himself. You are a one who—with one other or one hundred others or one million others—is presently showing the world what the face of Jesus is like. Your exact day today is your witness unto Him. Along with me—and a whole world of His disciples.

So let's bring it home, shall we?

Today, what if the most top-of-mind, totally engrossing thought in your head was this promise that He's with you, He's speaking, and, if you'll listen, He'll always lead you unto fellowship with Himself? What if you spent your day in fellowship with His Spirit—and with Him—and, whenever He asked you to, re-assembled His Body?

For remember: *You are one of the "two or three" that's necessary.*

And where that "two or three gather," *there He is.*

Your way through this day is the way He's showing the world *His Way. What an awesome opportunity to listen!*

Section Five

JESUS IS GIVING US HIS OWN INNER LIFE

Promise
20

*"The thief comes only to steal and kill and destroy;
I have come that they may have life, and have it to
the full."*

JOHN 10:10, NIV

Today, we're beginning a five-part section of promises that I've given the header of "Jesus Is Giving Us His Own Inner Life." It wasn't enough for Jesus to show us His life, to give His life to set us free, to come back to life, to ascend to Heaven for us, to send the Holy Spirit who was His life—no, He absolutely required the direct transmission of both the quality and quantity of heavenly life that filled every day of *His* earthly life. He would have us drawing from the same well every day. Nothing is meant to be any different for us than it was for Him.

So, we begin with His justly famous promise of His "life to the full."

To properly get at the infinite weightiness attached to taking on Jesus' own inner life, it's important to notice the inversion He's put in play. "The thief"—the evil one, the tempter, satan—is *not* the opposite of Himself; that would be giving satan far too much credit. "The thief" (this renegade upstart angel) "comes" (he plans, he travels, he arrives) "only" (he *only* has a single strategy with three intertwined tactical plans) "to steal and kill and destroy." He *only* wants to take away those pieces of life that tend toward connection with the Godhead. Thievery is his first line of attack there. And he *only* looks to bodily murder every single human alive. It would be the simplest thing for him to see every life extinguished outside of eternal salvation. And he *only*, in the absence of either stealing or outright murder, is perfectly happy with the outcome of pointless destruction. "The thief comes only to steal and kill and destroy"—anything outside these three tactics are activities *we* assign to satan. He is an uncomplicated spirit. His strategy and tactics are static.

But on the other hand, on the plane where human life is meant to be wrapped into the life of God, we find our wonderful Jesus: "I have come that they—*that you*—may have life, and have it to the full"—*just like He did*. If the evil one would rob us, Jesus of Nazareth would give to, grant us, everything that a Son of God gets. His inner life plan is to overwhelm our human sensibilities with draft after draft of the Holy Spirit, His life, His presence. Not a little drip-drop—*a flood* of His bestowal, His giving, of His own inner life!

And if the evil one would murder, Jesus would *be* murdered, *be* slain, so that the curse of death is swallowed up in life forever. He would *so* disarm our former fear of death and dying that life becomes the sweetest possible experience of communion *with* His life. Life that knows no earthly or heavenly end. Life that keeps on coming till we out-age the stars and sky.

Finally, if the evil one is busy with all kinds of destruction, Jesus is *infinitely more willing* to get down to all kinds of acts of *construction*. His is an inward ministry of building up—of setting foundations and footers in the inner life—so that we may take our place in the Household of God. Your life is being formed and fitted *perfectly, precisely, exactly* for the position it holds in the stonework of Heaven. The whole thing hinges upon the part for which He's shaping you; your inner life's formation is foundational to the work of the Way.

So, again, "I have come that they—*that you*—may have life, and have it to the full."

If your experience of this promise and its fruit has been of a limited nature to date, I'm encouraging you—*stick with it!* Stop perceiving that your self-limited portions of partaking of His life means that *He* is limited; you just haven't begun to feast yet. You haven't begun to possess what's properly yours; you've conflated less-than-full experience with a less-than-robust Life of your Savior.

Simply, don't do that. Or even *stop* doing that.

Instead, today, what if you said to Him, "Jesus, I want it all; I want everything on offer in this arrangement—Your gift of life, the life You gave, the life You'd build. Come and possess the fullness of my inner life. Come fully, Jesus, with the fullness of Your own life."

I'm promising you that He's faithful to fulfill that promise.

He promised it right here, didn't He?

Promise
21

*"I have told you these things so that you will be filled
with my joy. Yes, your joy will overflow!"*

JOHN 15:11, NLT

First off, the intended destination of this promise is joy—
to be filled with joy—in fact, to be filled with the very joy
of Jesus, which, by the way, overflows. To see no benefit in
the passing fancies that would seem to end in happiness (that
changeable quantity!); to instead be seeded deep, deep down in
the soil of your inner life with that springing-up, sprouting-up,
heavenly, earthly, celebratory, reality-reducing, true-reali-
ty-producing fruit of the Spirit that stands second in line only
to love itself.

I'm talking about *joy!*

To be filled with the joy of Jesus Himself. To overflow
with the natural joy of the Savior so that wherever we go the
sloshings and spillings of our cup of joy have incidentally covered and changed the places we depart from.

And this is, in fact, the kind of joy you've been promised!
The joy of Jesus that changes the world by changing hearts.

So, how do we get at this promise? If joy is the intended
destination, what is our line of approach?

Well, Jesus already told us: "I have told you *these things so that* you will be filled with My joy." The words of His Last Discourse on the night before the Cross, in the upper room and on the way to the Mount of Olives, are those "these things."

So, in chronological order, here are the wondrous words of Jesus—the "these things" that are intended to fill our hearts with His overflowing joy. I'd encourage you to slow down and really read the following words. These are the words with those most marvelous, straight-from-Jesus-to-you, personal, joyful benefits.

"Do you realise what I have just done for you [in washing your feet]? You call me 'teacher' and 'Lord' and you are quite right, for I am your teacher and your Lord. But if I, your teacher and Lord, have washed your feet, you must be ready to wash one another's feet. I have given you this as an example so that you may do as I have done. Believe me, the servant is not greater than his master and the messenger is not greater than the man who sent him. Once you have realised these things, you will find your happiness in doing them.

..."From now onwards, I shall tell you about things before they happen, so that when they do happen, you may believe that I am the one I claim to be. I tell you truly that anyone who accepts my messenger will be accepting me, and anyone who accepts me will be accepting the one who sent me.

...*"Now comes the glory of the Son of Man, and the glory of God in him! If God is glorified through him then God will glorify the Son of Man—and that without delay. Oh, my children, I am with you such a short time! You will look for me and I have to tell you as I told the Jews, 'Where I am going, you cannot follow.' Now I am giving you a new command—love one another. Just as I have loved you, so you must love one another. This is how all men will know that you are my disciples, because you have such love for one another.*

"You must not let yourselves be distressed—you must hold on to your faith in God and to your faith in me. There are many rooms in my Father's House. If there were not, should I have told you that I am going to prepare a place for you? It is true that I am going away to prepare a place for you, but it is just as true that I am coming again to welcome you into my own home, so that you may be where I am. You know where I am going and you know the way I am going to take.

...*"I myself am the road...and the truth and the life. No one approaches the Father except through me. If you had known who I am, you would have known my Father. From now on, you do know him and you have seen him.*

...*"The man who has seen me has seen the Father.... Do you not believe that I am in the Father and the Father is in me? The very words I say to you are not my own. It is the Father who lives in me who carries out his work through me. Do you believe me when I say that I am in the Father and the Father is in me? But if you cannot, then believe me because of what you see me do. I assure you that the man who believes in me will do the same things that I have done, yes, and he will do even greater things than these, for I am going away to the Father. Whatever you ask the Father in my name, I will do—that the Son may bring glory to the Father. And if you ask me anything in my name, I will grant it.*

"If you really love me, you will keep the commandments I have given you and I shall ask the Father to give you someone else to stand by you, to be with you always. I mean the Spirit of truth, whom the world cannot accept, for it can neither see nor recognise that Spirit. But you recognise him, for he is with you now and will be in your hearts. I am not going to leave you alone in the world—I am coming to you. In a very little while, the world will see me no more but you will see me, because I am really alive and you will be alive too. When that day come, you will realise that I am in my Father, that you are in me, and I am in you.

"Every man who knows my commandments and obeys them is the man who really loves me, and every man who really loves me will himself be loved by my Father, and I too will love him and make myself known to him.

…*"When a man loves me, he follows my teaching. Then my Father will love him, and we will come to that man and make our home within him. The man who does not really love me will not follow my teaching. Indeed, what you are hearing from me now is not really my saying, but comes from the Father who sent me.*

"I have said all this while I am still with you. But the one who is coming to stand by you, the Holy Spirit whom the Father will send in my name, will be your teacher and will bring to your minds all that I have said to you.

"I leave behind with you—peace; I give you my own peace and my gift is nothing like the peace of this world. You must not be distressed and you must not be daunted. You have heard me say, 'I am going away and I am coming back to you.' If you really loved me, you would be glad because I am going to my Father, for my Father is greater than I. And I have told you of it now, before it happens, so that when it does happen, your faith in me will not be shaken. I shall not be able to talk much longer to you for the spirit that rules this world is coming very close. He has no hold over me, but I go on my way to show the world that I love the Father and do what he sent me to do" (John 13:12–14:31 PNT).

"I am the true vine, and My Father is the vinedresser. Every branch in Me that does not bear fruit He takes away; and every branch that bears fruit He prunes,

that it may bear more fruit. You are already clean because of the word which I have spoken to you. Abide in Me, and I in you. As the branch cannot bear fruit of itself, unless it abides in the vine, neither can you, unless you abide in Me.

"I am the vine, you are the branches. He who abides in Me, and I in him, bears much fruit; for without Me you can do nothing. If anyone does not abide in Me, he is cast out as a branch and is withered; and they gather them and throw them into the fire, and they are burned. If you abide in Me, and My words abide in you, you will ask what you desire, and it shall be done for you. By this My Father is glorified, that you bear much fruit; so you will be My disciples.

"As the Father loved Me, I also have loved you; abide in My love. If you keep My commandments, you will abide in My love, just as I have kept My Father's commandments and abide in His love" (John 15:1-10 NKJV).

"I have told you these things so that you will be filled with my joy. Yes, your joy will overflow!" (John 15:11 NLT).

Yes, Jesus, it will—and it already does.

Promise
22

"Peace I leave with you; my peace I give to you. Not as the world gives do I give to you. Let not your hearts be troubled, neither let them be afraid."

JOHN 14:27, ESV

It's perfect that the English Standard Version has taken this series of Greek words, as spoken by Jesus in Aramaic, and split them into three short declarative sentences in English. Why? Because the first sentence tells us of our limitless perfect inheritance, bestowed upon us by our Savior; the second tells us precisely why that so deeply matters; and the third, with the added emphasis of coming as a commandment, tells us what we must do, with regard to our inheritance and the world, to properly guard it till the day we die.

Shall we give a closer look to all three?

I want you to imagine Jesus, just the way you imagine Him. See Him in your mind's eye with all the details that come along with that—the look of His clothing, the set of His shoulders, the look in His eyes and on His face as He leans closer to you. He is sitting in a room where, just a few minutes ago, He'd stooped at your feet and washed and dried them; now He's been speaking to you very directly. Something in His eyes says that all these words are a valediction—a sort of farewell—like a father preparing to make his final earthly departure. You find your heart confused, sad. Why is He suddenly taking on a tone like this?

Then His features soften; His eyes gloss over with tears. "Peace I leave with you," He says, "*My* peace I give to you." In the last three years of following after Him, you have seen the nature of that peace; scenes begin to occur to your memory. Of the crush of the crowds pressing against Him from all sides. Of the approach of Legion, the man possessed by a thousand spirits. Of the night before that—His waking in the storm and standing up against the gunwale and pronouncing "Hush" into the night. Of the constant attacks of the Pharisees and Sadducees. Of the rumors of the fury of Herod. Of the whispering of the authorities unto the Romans. Of the day, even, when He'd cleared the Temple.

The peace He is leaving you, *His* peace that He says He gives, is the most remarkable power you have ever seen. Jesus' peace is not the absence of action—a vacuum where no problems may enter—it is a conquering force that dominates every situation. You have seen the way His peace can be as quiet as the light mellowing at dusk; you have seen it rise to confront all evil in its darkness. The peace that Jesus gives you, on this night and forever, is the ability to abide in Him no matter what. It's the ability to conquer fear with love, hate with goodness, lack with abundance, death with life. Nothing can stand against the peace of Jesus.

He goes on: "Not as the world gives do I give to you." And it's easy for you to understand what the world gives. Your whole human life has shown you the limits and restrictions it would like to offer you. Fear for your daily bread and drink; fear for your safety and security; a sense of need and constant lack when it comes to love, care, purpose. Every day to wake into the reality that it's all like a house of cards—everything hinging upon itself—and, if a single wrong move is made, *it's over.* That is what the world gives to you. What you already know of it is already enough.

And what Jesus gives you—His peace—is *nothing like the weight and worry and woe of this world.* In fact, His peace is the weapon that conquers it all. His peace is the answer to your every earth-bound question.

Then His features suddenly harden—flame with a fire— and He leans forward and grabs your shoulders with His hands: "Let not your heart be troubled, neither let it be afraid." *Let not. Do not let.* Do not ever find yourself a party to the world's subtle attacks; *you now have My peace.* Do not ever countenance any thought that digs beneath the value of the Kingdom of Heaven; *you now have My peace.* Do not let your own human heart ever speak of insurmountable troubles; *you now have My peace.* Do not be afraid; let no fear become your master; *you now have My peace.*

Then, all at once, He leans away from you, His face breaks into a smile; He is done with the speaking of this part of His will and testament. You, an inheritor of His whole heavenly Kingdom, have been bequeathed His own personal peace— forever. And it's nothing like the world gives; actually, it *conquers* all the warfare and strife that the world offers.

And your only job today and forever to enjoy this inheritance—the only task that's needed to properly take hold of it?

"Let not your heart be troubled" and "neither let it be afraid," at all, ever. Which—just in case that action and requirement sounds daunting to you—is guaranteed by His peace that's already yours.

What a truly perfect Friend we always have in Jesus!

Hadn't you heard?

This Friend *is* the Prince of Peace!

Promise
23

"These things I have spoken to you, so that in Me you may have peace. In the world you have tribulation, but take courage; I have overcome the world."

JOHN 16:33, NASB

Let's make sure we understand *how* Jesus overcame the world so that we may personally take courage and, in that way, *walk right through* the tribulation the world offers us. Do you have an immediate explanation for these words of His? If you and I were together, sitting across a table from one another, and I asked you, *"How* did He overcome the world?"—what would you say? Can you succinctly explain His all-conquering, world-shifting strategy so that another person may experience the peace His Gospel is meant to bring?

In my reading this week, I came across this beautiful explanation:

Now may the God of peace [there's that word again] who brought back from the dead that great shepherd of the sheep, our Lord Jesus, by the blood of the everlasting agreement, equip you thoroughly for the doing of his will! May he effect in you everything that pleases him through Jesus Christ, to whom be glory for ever and ever (Hebrews 13:20-21 PNT).

Aren't those words encouraging—and inspiring?

The God of *peace*—the peace that Jesus promises here, again—is the very One whose power resurrected our great Good Shepherd. Jesus' blood is the sealing of the everlasting agreement, the New Covenant, and its all-sufficiency is the power by which our lives may be equipped for doing His perfect will. And it is God who personally effects in us *everything that personally pleases Himself* by giving us the inner experience of the presence of His Son, Jesus. The God of peace—the peace of God, that eternal attribute of His wondrous glory—will lead our lives in a way that perfectly conquers all tribulation, calls us to take courage, and in the end, with Him, will overcome the world and its ways.

Which brings us back to the first sentence of today's promise.

"These things," He says—and here we are again in the words of the Last Discourse, by the way—"I have spoken to you."

Why?

"So that in Me you may have peace." That's His stated intention, in these words. It's Jesus' purpose to fill our hearts with His peace—the peace of the God who is peace—so that, once again, we may walk through tribulation, take courage, overcome.

And how does He plan to invest us with that peace?

In the very same manner as He did day before yesterday: "*These things* I have spoken to you."

These things!

Shall we consider all the "these things" He's talking about in the latter half of the Last Discourse? Shall we listen to the rest of the words from that night before the Cross that are the "these things" Jesus is specifically referring to here?

Well, here we go.

> *"This is my commandment: that you love each other as I have loved you. There is no greater love than this— that a man should lay down his life for his friends. You are my friends if you do what I tell you to do. I shall not call you servants any longer, for a servant does not share his master's confidence. No, I call you friends, now, because I have told you everything that I have heard from the Father.*
>
> *"It is not that you have chosen me; but it is I who have chosen you. I have appointed you to go and bear fruit that will be lasting; so that whatever you ask the Father in my name, he will give it to you.*
>
> *"This I command you, love one another! If the world hates you, you know that it hated me first. If you belonged to the world, the world would love its own. But because you do not belong to the world and I have chosen you out of it, the world will hate you. Do you remember what I said to you, 'The servant is not greater than his master'? If they have persecuted me, they will persecute you as well, but if they have followed my teaching, they will also follow yours. They will do all these things to you as my disciples because*

they do not know the one who sent me. If I had not come and spoken to them, they would not have been guilty of sin, but now they have no excuse for their sin. The man who hates me, hates my Father as well. If I had not done among them things that no other man has ever done, they would not have been guilty of sin, but as it is they have seen and they have hated both me and my Father. Yet this only fulfils what is written in their Law—'They hated me without a cause.'

"But when the helper comes, that is, the Spirit of truth, who comes from the Father and whom I myself will send to you from the Father, he will speak plainly about me. And you yourselves will also speak plainly about me for you have been with me from the first.

"I am telling you this now so that your faith in me may not be shaken. They will excommunicate you from their synagogues. Yes, the time is coming when a man who kills you will think he is thereby serving God! They will act like this because they have never had any true knowledge of the Father or of me, but I have told you all this so that when the time comes for it to happen you may remember that I told you about it. I have not spoken like this to you before, because I have been with you; but now the time has come for me to go away to the one who sent me. None of you asks me, 'Where are you going?' That is because you are so distressed at what I have told you. Yet I am telling you the simple truth when I assure you that it is a good

thing for you that I should go away. For if I did not go away, the divine helper would not come to you. But if I go, then I will send him to you. When he comes, he will convince the world of the meaning of sin, of true goodness and of judgment. He will expose their sin because they do not believe in me; he will reveal true goodness for I am going away to the Father and you will see me no longer; and he will show them the meaning of judgment, for the spirit which rules this world will have been judged.

"I have much more to tell you but you cannot bear it now. Yet when that one I have spoken to you about comes—the Spirit of truth—he will guide you into everything that is true. For he will not be speaking of his own accord but exactly as he hears, and he will inform you about what is to come. He will bring glory to me for he will draw on my truth and reveal it to you. Whatever the Father possesses is also mine; that is why I tell you that he will draw on my truth and will show it to you.

"In a little while you will not see me any longer, and again, in a little while you will see me.

..."I tell you truly that you are going to be both sad and sorry while the world is glad. Yes, you will be deeply distressed, but your pain will turn into joy. When a woman gives birth to a child, she certainly knows pain when her time comes. Yet as soon as she has given birth to the child, she no longer remembers her agony for joy that a man has been born into the

world. Now you are going through pain, but I shall see you again and your hearts will thrill with joy—the joy that no one can take away from you—and on that day you will not ask me any questions.

"I assure you that whatever you ask the Father he will give you in my name. Up to now you have asked nothing in my name; ask now, and you will receive, that your joy may be overflowing.

"I have been speaking to you in parables—but the time is coming to give up parables and tell you plainly about the Father. When that time comes, you will make your requests to him in my own name, for I need make no promise to plead to the Father for you, for the Father himself loves you, because you have loved me and have believed that I came from God. Yes, I did come from the Father and I came into the world. Now I leave the world behind and return to the Father (John 15:12–16:28 PNT).

"Behold, an hour is coming, and has already come, for you to be scattered, each to his own home, and to leave Me alone; and yet I am not alone, because the Father is with Me. These things I have spoken to you, so that in Me you may have peace. In the world you have tribulation, but take courage; I have overcome the world" (John 16:32-33 NASB).

Yes, You have, Jesus.

Yes, *You have!*

And thank You, Jesus, for Your perfect peace.

Promise
24

*"Blessed are the poor in spirit, for theirs is the king-
dom of heaven. Blessed are those who mourn, for they
shall be comforted. Blessed are the meek, for they shall
inherit the earth. Blessed are those who hunger and
thirst for righteousness, for they shall be satisfied.
Blessed are the merciful, for they shall receive mercy.
Blessed are the pure in heart, for they shall see God.
Blessed are the peacemakers, for they shall be called
sons of God. Blessed are those who are persecuted for
righteousness' sake, for theirs is the kingdom of heaven.
Blessed are you when others revile you and persecute
you and utter all kinds of evil against you falsely on
my account. Rejoice and be glad, for your reward is
great in heaven, for so they persecuted the prophets
who were before you."*

MATTHEW 5:3-12, ESV

I've often noticed that sermons about these words, the
Beatitudes, tend to focus on their middle clause—the spiritual protagonist of each state of blessedness. So, over eight
or nine weeks, a pastor might cleverly extrapolate upon the
meaning of *being* "poor in spirit" or "meek," *being* one of "the

peacemakers" or "the pure in heart." Which, let's be honest, can end up feeling like a laundry list for a number of ways you *aren't*—another reminder that the so-called "Christian life" is very different-seeming from the one you're living. There's nothing better than finishing a book or sermon series feeling fairly convinced that there's no practical way you're ever going to be able to do what's been described, right? Nothing like that feeling of, "Then why try?"

So, let's take a different approach today.

Why are the people described by Jesus here so "blessed"? Is it because they *set out* to be a such-and-such sort of person or because of what they now *receive*? Did a man, woman, or child strive to be a person "who mourns" because they expected something—some reward for that activity? Probably not. Are people getting out of bed and *trying* to be "persecuted for righteousness' sake" because they're excited about the back end, their spiritual bottom line in this? Frankly, I hope not.

Instead, consider Jesus' words in the manner that makes them understandable; then we'll circle back to make the promise in all this far clearer. Take a read:

- Blessed are those who possess the Kingdom of Heaven.

- Blessed are those who will be comforted.

- Blessed are those who will inherit the earth.

- Blessed are those who will be satisfied.

- Blessed are the ones who will receive mercy.

- Blessed are those who will see God.

- Blessed are those who will be called sons of God.

- Blessed, again, are those who possess the Kingdom of Heaven.

- Blessed are those who may rejoice and be glad because their reward in Heaven is great, for they've been treated like the prophets of old.

Do you see how clearly the blessedness of those blessings now actually starts to sound like a series of clear blessings? If you look at the ending of each statement, you find the blessed *destination* where Jesus lands each person described in the Beatitudes.

Now let's look at those middle clauses, shall we?

Slowly, I want you to read the descriptions Jesus gives of the *type* of person who will be blessed in the above manner. You've read these many a time—I know that. But I want you to read again, and slowly, and think of *Who*, precisely, each of these sound like. Consider:

- Poor in spirit.

- Ready to mourn alongside of.

- Meek. Gentle.

- Hungry and thirsty for righteousness.

- Merciful. Full of mercy.

- Pure in heart.

- A peacemaker. A literal fashioner of peace.

- One persecuted for the sake of righteousness.

- One reviled, persecuted, and against whom all kinds of evil were uttered.

Does any of that sound strangely familiar?

What's so glorious about the promise of the Beatitudes is that that central position, that middle clause, *is none other than Jesus Himself.*

He is poor in spirit—humble-hearted in the eyes of God and man. *He* is hungry and thirsty to see the righteousness of Heaven alive upon earth. *He* is the One whose heart is full of mercy for all. *He* is the peacemaker whose own body and blood paid the price to end the war of wars.

So, if we possess ourselves of the presence, experience, person, and personality of Jesus of Nazareth, we possess the Beatitudes. *We* get to inherit the Kingdom of Heaven. *We* find ourselves contented, perfectly satisfied. *We* get to receive the wondrous mercy of Heaven. *We* have the opportunity, today, to live and love and be and become the sons and daughters of God.

The promise offered up throughout the Beatitudes is the promise that we shall inherit all the beautiful, beatific blessednesses He speaks of.

How?

By being, ourselves, perfect?

By figuring out how to slide into that middle-clause slot?

By somehow perfectly "gaming the system" and figuring out ways to unexpectedly become something totally different than we are ourselves?

How's that gone for you, so far?

No, the perfect promise of Jesus in His speaking of His Beatitudes is that by abiding in Him, He comes and lives this life in us. No longer do we operate under a system of religious law where all our lives are given to perfectly understanding and obeying one overall Law.

You and I follow *this Man!*

The One who says, "Abide in Me, and I will abide in you."

The One whose natural nature is everything offered in the course of the Beatitudes; the One whose living of that life in us is the bridge between the "Blessed" and the blessednesses.

Today's promise is *possession* of the Beatitudes.

Today.

In Jesus.

Section Six

JESUS IS ALWAYS WITH US

Promise
25

"I am the light of the world. Whoever follows me will never walk in darkness, but will have the light of life."

JOHN 8:12, NIV

Allegorically speaking, imagine waking up in total pitch-black darkness—even though you are fairly certain that it should be light out already. Your body has every indication that it's already morning time. Yet opening your eyes—total darkness; nothing can be seen.

You rise to your feet and—*oh!*—*hit your head!* The ceiling overhead is lower than your full height. You reach up with your hands and feel along its surface; it is rough and craggy, rocky, moist to the touch. *Are you in a cave?* Have you somehow awakened deep within the recesses of the belly of the earth? Your heart starts racing at the very thought!

You try to move around now, to feel things out. The inky blackness of the darkness starts to feel like it's suffocating your sense of vision; you're fighting off that feeling of panic.

That's when you *think* you see the strangest sight—*is it a sight? are you seeing it?*—a range of (are they?) colors against a wall in the distant distance. It almost looks like bars of color—bars of faintly colored glowings—that are dimly *almost* lighting the wall in that other space. You try to make your way there, to see this *almost* light—especially in the beauty of its colored arrangement—but then it disappears. It's gone.

But before you even feel the pangs of disappointment, there is suddenly *actual* light, *actual* experience of brightness, coming from somewhere behind you. As fast as you can you have wheeled around, sought with all the intensity of your eyesight to capture this light that was coming from behind and—*oh no!*—it's not real light. Immediately, you can tell that it's indirect. You can tell the look of light reflecting from a mirror or a pool or a glass. Somehow, a light is shining—*but not right here.* And then, just like that, it disappears entirely.

In the space between your panic and pain, you begin to walk, hands out, groping, feeling for anything that will you give a clue to escape. Around you, there are stalactites, stalagmites, rocks, and outcroppings everywhere; you are bruised with the sheer work of walking. You are, almost, just about to give up. You are nearly, just in a second, ready to sit down and cry.

Then, reaching out, you feel something warm. Your hands start to warm at the touch of it, the feel of it. You run your hands along the length of this warm, quite warm figure. *Is it a figure? Is it a person?* No, it's just a stone. Just a stone stuck in place like all the others. Warm to the touch, but just a stone.

If you're not asking yourself, *Why in the world is he writing about this imaginary cave?* then I'd almost have to guess you haven't been paying attention at all!

Here's why I'm writing about this allegorical cave.

The experience of waking up every morning in the pitch darkness of a cave *is the actual experience of everyone who doesn't know Jesus.* They may *think* they have some experience of life, living, love, and light; they may be ready to *passionately argue* the sentence I just wrote.

But if Jesus is "the light of the world," the defeater of "darkness," the "light of life," then logically speaking, His absence is also the presence of darkness. And spiritually speaking, if you yourself made any sort of attempt at figuring out life before you actually met Him, then you know the darkness that came before. You know precisely what I'm talking about.

But what about the common graces? a more relaxed believer might say.

Yes—and what about the beauties I constantly see? an unbeliever might add.

I'd remind you of the cave, I'd reply to both. I'd remind you of my little allegory before.

Without direct experience of Jesus, any seeming experience of light is only refraction or dispersion or reflection. The modern world that appears to be so lighted is only the diffusive, diffused, collective experience of seeing the colors born from His light's *dispersal.* They are broken out prismatically, shade by shade. It is second-hand grace, and the world can't live by that.

Or, the world sees puzzling reflections that hit their hearts with wild fragments of light; they flash and shimmer and surprise and startle them. They try to turn and see this seeming light as fast as possible. But it's not enough, it's indirect, it seems to flee.

And then, saddest of all, after such secondary refraction and reflection, light is only able to be experienced in one other way—absorption. The saddest of all are all those bearers of the name of "Christian" who would *absorb* the light of Jesus, be warmed, and yet let themselves be turned to stone. Be "immovable," yes. And yet totally unmoved.

My friend, I'm speaking somewhat challengingly about this promise because the *promise* of this promise is the way it's meant to change our hearts forever. You might recall that this Jesus, this "light of the world," also earlier called His *followers* the "light of the world" (Matt. 5:14). But did you know that this was the only one of the "I am" statements that Jesus also pronounced to be the definition of *our* lives? And, did you know that the only way we're able to be "lights of the world" is to be constantly lighted and personally lit by the "light of the world"? Did you know that how this promise fills your life with light and love and heavenly living is by *practical application*? If my allegory of the cave does anything worthwhile today, I hope it spurs you to be down in the darkness *with the light*—setting others free.

Because the only way to *not* be negatively refractive, reflective, or absorptive of the light of Heaven is to be filled to overflowing.

And the only way to test the limits of His light amidst the darkness of this world is to literally be in the darkness of this world with His light.

This promise is a provocation, in my mind. The world's darkness should provoke you into action.

Because Jesus is the "light of the world," the One with whom you'll "never walk in darkness," will *you* be the "light of the world" He's promised you to be?

He's literally, personally handed you this promise and the chance to co-operate in one of His "I ams." Today, will you be the "light of the world" *with Him*?

Promise
26

"Call upon Me in the day of trouble; I will deliver you, and you shall glorify Me."

PSALM 50:15, NKJV

If you were raised in a fairly old-fashioned Christian home and I should say to you, "Hey, what is the chief end of man?" do you know what you would respond? Well if, like me, you'd been brought up having to learn questions and answers from the Westminster Shorter Catechism, it would come like clockwork: *"Man's chief end is to glorify God and enjoy Him forever."*

I've always appreciated that answer, even though I'm not a big fan of rote learning requirements in matters pertaining to Jesus, because, in its two-part formula, glorifying God proceeds naturally into the experience of getting to enjoy the goodnesses of God everlastingly. In essence, if we would be *serious* about our desire to enjoy God forever—to really relish what's ours—then we must *begin* with learning to glorify Him.

Which brings us back to the grandeur of today's promise.

Did you notice how it too is like a formula? How A + B = C; and, in fact, did you notice what that resulting C is? Just like my Westminster Shorter Catechism answer #1, the answer is *to glorify God.*

Now, let's connect the dots.

"Call upon Me in the day of trouble," He says to us. The day of trouble—do you recognize the sort of day that might be? Is there any chance that today, in actual actuality, might be a day wherein you encounter a couple troubles in your transit? Do you think there's slightly a possibility that someone in your life—could be an enemy, could be a friend—might not let this day pass easily for you? Do you think a moment might come today when, thinking back, you remember the words on this page right now, and think, "A-ha! *This* is a day of trouble"?

Then, thinking that, what are you meant to do next?

"Call upon *Me*," the Lord tells us.

Because, then, what will He do?

"I will deliver you." Simple as that. Isn't that absolutely wonderful? Right now, I'm writing out this sentence at 6:33 in the morning, having only the vaguest idea what the day might hold, but I know the One who spoke these words is with me. And He already knows *exactly* what this day will hold. He knows about that text that'll come, or that email that'll bother my mid-morning, or that unexpected bill that'll arrive in the afternoon mail. He knows already what I'll end up having for lunch. He knows what Jenny and I might watch when the day is done. He knows how I will sleep tonight; He knows how *tomorrow's* meditation will get written; He knows everything about every breath of my every minute.

And so, finding myself in any minute, any breath when the day has become a "day of trouble," I may call upon Him— *and be delivered*. Simple as that. And I'll say it again: Isn't that wonderful? What a wonder that the peace and joy and courage that guarded the steps of Jesus are the same peace and joy and courage that may attend my steps. If *I* call, He *will* answer. If *I'm* in the midst of trouble today, *He* will deliver me.

And not only may I call on Him in the day of trouble, not only will He then deliver me, He has also given me a corollary purpose in this whole arrangement: "and you shall glorify Me." Having become a person who's perfectly welcome to "Call upon Him in the day of trouble," having experienced His promised deliverance, what else should I do? Naturally, I'll be so delighted *at* the glorious opportunity I had to call on the very God of Heaven, so elated *within* His immediate practical deliverance that, quite frankly, all I'll want to do is find a way to glorify Him with the rest of the day ahead.

So here's some questions for you as you're living your life today:

Do you want to enjoy God?

Do you believe you should glorify Him?

Do you want to know that deliverance is always at your door?

Are you fairly certain that, like I wrote before, this day—*any day*—might yield its own share of troubles?

Then, remember—He has promised you that if you call, He will deliver, and He'll give you opportunity for glorifying Him. And if you glorify Him, assuming those wily men at Westminster weren't totally blowing smoke, then you're on the road to everlasting enjoyment.

These are the sorts of promise formulas I can get excited about!

Promise 27

"This is my command—be strong and courageous! Do not be afraid or discouraged. For the Lord your God is with you wherever you go."

JOSHUA 1:9, NLT

Here's a picture: Imagine standing on the wide, sweeping plains on the west side of the Jordan River, listening to the sound of the wind whistling through the river rushes. Behind you, a few hundred yards away, sleep the hundreds of thousands of people you have just become the leader for; you have only just become their leader in place of the only leader they've ever known. You're standing in the darkness, by yourself, listening to the whistling of the wind, wondering how you'll ever accomplish the next day. Before you stretches the land that, all throughout your life, you've heard is yours; forty years before, you'd even spied it out. You have personally tasted the sweetness of its fruit, seen the beauty of its mountains and valleys, observed the mighty fortresses you'll have to take to take it.

All in all, you are scared. And excited.

But, really and truly, scared.

Looking back, you begin studying the swirling and flaring and expanding and contracting movements of the pillar of fire that hangs just this side of the camp. It's funny. There are times, *like right now*, when it's become easy to forget the power of the presence of God; when that great theophany fades into the commonplace. You walk a little closer, opening out the fullness of your spirit, wishing you could just hear a voice to help you know how to…

"Moses my servant is dead," the Fire suddenly speaks directly to you.

You are already on your face on the ground.

Within a few moments, the words of today's promise become the centerpiece of the command of God that is spoken to you on behalf of all the people: *"This is my command—be strong and courageous! Do not be afraid or discouraged. For the Lord your God is with you wherever you go."*

When you rise to your feet, when you look back toward the promise of the Promised Land standing before you, this command and its promise now leads the way.

"God is with you" now leads the way.

Now, here's another picture.

Imagine standing within the open, unknown sweeps of the dawning of a new day, listening to the sound of your schedule, plans, expectations, and worries for it. Around you in every home, on every street, all over the whole world live the billions of people you have been called to serve; you have been called to serve them by the One who came not to *be* served, but to serve, and to give His life as a ransom for many (see Matt. 20:28). You're standing in the daylight or the darkness by yourself, listening to the beatings of your heart, wondering how you'll ever accomplish this day. Before you stretch the realities of Heaven that, all throughout your life, you've heard to be yours; here and there, in reality, you've actually even spied some out. You have personally tasted the sweetness of its fruit, seen the beauty of its peaks and hidden places, observed the mighty fortresses by which it protects your every day.

All in all, you are still a little uncertain. Excited, yes.

But, really and truly, uncertain.

Taking a moment, you begin remembering the swirling and flaring and firing and calming movements of the Holy Spirit who lives within you. It's funny. There are times, like right now, when it's easy to forget the power of the presence of God; when His great theophany fades into the common-place. So you focus a little bit closer, opening out the fullness of your spirit, wishing you could just hear a voice to help you know how to...

"Jesus, my Servant, has died for you," the Spirit reminds you.

You should already be on your face on the ground.

And within a few moments, the words of today's promise become the centerpiece of the command of God that is spoken to you on behalf of the whole world: *"This is my command— be strong and courageous! Do not be afraid or discouraged. For the Lord your God is with you wherever you go."*

When you rise to your feet, when you look back toward the day, toward the promise of Heaven standing before you, this command and its promise must now lead the way.

God within you must now lead the way.

Are you ready, now, to go?

Promise
28

"All these things my hand has made, and so all these things came to be, declares the Lord. But this is the one to whom I will look: he who is humble and contrite in spirit and trembles at my word."

ISAIAH 66:2, ESV

Nearly every afternoon for the last almost-eight years I've lived in this house, I walk out the door, pass through the gate, turn up the street, and begin one of my looping dog walks up Cheyenne Cañon. Our canyon is this marvelous, tree-filled, jagged cut into the front range of the Rocky Mountains; a little stream, Cheyenne Creek, flows right down through the middle. And as I make my way upcanyon, here's what I pay attention to:

Ahead, above, a pair of peaks, with a graceful saddle between them, covered with a bristling spine of pines swaying in the breeze.

To my left, the flowing of the stream, over and around rocks and boulders, sometimes tumbling down over small, lovely-sounding waterfalls.

Around me, the mixture of the pines and cottonwoods, standing straight and tall, bending a little if the wind over the mountains is blowing that day.

In the canopy of those trees, the movements of the birds— lark buntings, ravens, sparrows, woodpeckers, occasionally a red-tailed hawk.

If I happen to be going a little farther, up to the gates of the tourist attraction at the southwest edge of the canyon, Seven Falls, I get into one of my favorite stretches. Here, you are looking up through a different set of mountains into a back country full of different peaks, different stands of trees, different unknowns. I love the feeling of looking up and past those distant ranges of peaks into wildernesses where, probably, not a single person is. On other days when I've climbed a particular peak in this section—Mt. Muscoco—I've just sat and sat and looked out over those distant stretches.

Imagine yourself sitting there with me.

Imagine if you and I were together on one of my walks.

With us, of course, would be Jesus, the Father, the Holy Spirit, and together they could say to us: "All these things My hand has made, and so all these things came to be." That pair of peaks ahead of us—*They made it.* The rippling sound of the stream flowing past us—*They made it.* The movements of the slender pines and stout spreading cottonwoods in the breeze— *They made all of those.* The sounds of the birds singing, the way they wheel and dance upon wings—*They made each and every one of them.* In fact, the way your body allows your legs to propel you forward, step after step—*They made you.* This wonderful Trio of perfectly interconnected personalities who are One in every way—*They made everything.*

All these things Their hand has made, and so all these things came to be.

What I appreciate about the wording of today's promise is how, in light of the facts I've just laid out, we are given a chance to personally respond. *We* are the people who may humble themselves, pursue contrition of spirit, learn to tremble at God's word—there are things you and I can do today. We can walk into every situation and look for ways to consciously humble our minds and hearts in the presence of both God and man. We can be reminded of our constant need of forgiveness, by both God and man, and seek the way of release through openhearted confession. We can open up our most precious possession—the pages of Scripture—and see what adventure the Lord would like to take us on.

Why?

Because toward the humble, contrite, trembling-at-the-Word man, woman, or child, we've been promised that that Lord "will look." He will consciously turn His gaze—the very eyes that first looked upon all His hand had made—and enjoy the sight of *you.* He will be *with* you, observing you. He will take *great delight* in His intimate fellowship with you. What a wonder that the all-powerful, glorious God of the universe is just on pins and needles for His next time together with you.

Isn't that a joyous thought for today?

Our opportunity, in the face of the God who created every landscape we behold, is to offer up *our* inner landscape to Him.

He has created mountains—*we may bring Him humility.* He pours water down the streambeds—*we, contrition.* He causes swaying in the tall trees—*we may tremble at His wondrous Word.* Every mighty call that His creation sends forth to our hearts may be answered in our hearts with the offering up of our own inner life.

If you desire intimate fellowship with our God, perfect union with the Godhead, pay attention today to all His creation's glories around you. This is the God you serve and you know and *may know ever better* as you bring Him the fullness of all that's inside you.

It has been promised.

Promise
29

"I will instruct you and teach you in the way which you should go; I will counsel you with My eye upon you."

PSALM 32:8, NASB

These promises are so absolutely, preposterously wonderful that I find it necessary to break them down, and amplify them, in their component parts. Humor me for a moment:

- *I*—the Father. The Son. The Spirit. The Trinity. The Unity that is the Godhead.

- *will*—the most steadfast, positive word in the whole language of promises;

- *instruct you*—advise you, disclose to you, direct you, acquaint you with;

- *and*—there's still more!

- *teach you in*—disciple you in, demonstrate for you, initiate you into, prepare you unequivocally for;

- *the way*—the Way who is a Man we know, Jesus;

YESTERDAY, TODAY & FOREVER

- *[in] which you should go*—the only Way. The Way that is synonymous with Truth and Life. The Way that leads directly, today and forever, into the presence of our heavenly Father.

- *I*—that same Father. His Son. His Spirit. The Trinity. The Unity that is the Godhead.

- *will*—again, that most steadfast, positive word in the whole language of promises;

- *counsel you*—advocate for you, exhort you, guide you, suggest to you, charge you;

- *with My eye upon you*—the individual Persons and Personalities of the Godhead—Father, Son, and Spirit—will turn upon Their throne. They will incline Their gaze in your direction. They will focus Their attention upon you. They will affectionately, lovingly, adoringly keep Their eye upon you, even while They're counseling you. They will extend Their hand of power and, pointing, help you understand the precise path you are meant to be walking. They will teach you of that path, leaving nothing at all to chance, and instruct you regarding its meaning and purpose.

So it is promised.

And so your God—Father, Son, and Spirit—*will* do. Nothing will be left undone or unsaid. You are the receiver of all these promises.

My friends, listening, hearing them, hearing me get a little carried away with their amplification—doesn't the whole of our earthly life come into a more brilliant focus? The God of Heaven and earth has personally guaranteed that it's *His* job to instruct, teach, and counsel you along the Way. He has not only *twice* said, "I will"—not only *tripled* down on the type of personal instruction He's offering—the whole thing will be eye to eye! Again, it's the Father, Son, and Holy Spirit promising that, with Their perfect eye upon your life, you *will* get the teaching you need. You *will* be discipled directly by the Spirit. You will know all you need to follow Jesus.

Can I invite you to take a deep breath and let it out, right now? (Really. Do it.)

He is with you today. His eye is upon you. He will instruct you. And teach you. He delights to personally counsel you.

So let's give our day to taking advantage of the nearness of our God and of His personal instruction—and see what happens.

I bet you'll have some tales to tell.

Promise
30

"I will never fail you. I will never abandon you."

HEBREWS 13:5, NLT

I take delivery every day of the *Wall Street Journal*, and it's one of my post-dropping-the-kids-at-school, pre-diving-into-the-work-of-the-day, personal rituals to make my way through its pages and read from its particular perspective. Typically—before the season in which I'm writing these words—the writings would be an international mélange of good and bad news; lots of interesting upsides and, to counterbalance, plenty of pretty bad downsides. But lately, with the world in the state it's in, with all the fear and uncertainty swirling around, with "sides" starting to arise about efficacies of treatment and realities of risk, I would describe the outlook of a daily *WSJ* perusal as:

Chaos.

Pandemonium.

Pure fear.

With no ready answers in sight.

As we prepare to finish our thirty days together in these meditations upon His promises, may I redirect your attention for a minute or two? I want you to actually be where

I'm talking about—in chaos, pandemonium, fear—but then I want you to understand how you can properly reorient your attentions. I want to show you a physical move you can literally make. I want to focus both our hearts upon the promise you just read.

Imagine it is night on the water. You are sitting in a thirty-foot boat surrounded by a vast sea. The stars sparkle overhead. The skies are mostly black. Just a few wisps of clouds catch the light of the moon. You are sitting forward on a bench, listening to the lapping of the water against the hull of the boat. Around you sit the other friends with whom you launched the boat earlier, just before the arrival of sunset, twilight, dusk.

Your state of mind is probably like the state of mind of the *Wall Street Journal*'s headlines *before* the pandemic—a mixture of basic ups and downs. Perhaps that day was good; you are feeling good. Perhaps that day was a little rougher; you are feeling down. Either way, your grown-up sense is telling you that, regardless of today, tomorrow is still coming; that every day holds potential for positive change. You are thinking ahead to what the weekend will hold, or of that friend you'd like to see, or of that...

What just happened?

Suddenly, a contrary wind has fouled the sails, twirling them till they're nearly tearing of their own accord, and the seas around you are beginning to toss like you're floating in a boiling cauldron. The boom is swinging side to side; you and your friends are ducking, trying to stay below its out-of-control movements. Others are on their hands and knees with buckets and bowls, trying to bail the water over the side before more gets spit in. The sound of the wind is deafening; water *slaps* against your face. Where just before your mood had been arranged within you in accordance with the past day, now it's moment-to-moment responding to these new stimuli:

Chaos.

Pandemonium.

Pure fear.

With no ready answers in sight.

My friend, if you're tracking with the narrative moment from the Gospels I'm trying to bring to light in your imagination, then you also know the most cogent detail: *Jesus, asleep in the stern.* And so imagine, now, you're looking over your shoulder, seeing Him back there on the cushion asleep, rolling and rising with the roll and rise of the storm swell.

This is your moment of decision on that night. This is your moment of decision in the midst of a global crisis.

Do you believe that, sleeping or not, visible or seemingly invisible, whether in bow or stern, the presence of Jesus is simply enough? Do you believe that His presence with you, storm or not, up or down, then or now, is absolutely all you need to transit this day?

Do you believe in Jesus?

And, believing—whether you're in calm or chaos, wealth or lack, peace or fear, readiness or shock—what will you do next? Will you rush to the stern, shake Him awake, accuse Him of an uncaring sleepiness, and try to force His hand into the deliverance you *think* you require? Will you shout in His

YESTERDAY, TODAY & FOREVER

face, "Jesus, don't You care that we're drowning?" when, in truth, you haven't even started to begin to *begin* to drown? You're still in the boat, aren't you? And you're looking into the face of Jesus!

Or, seeing the storm, feeling its fear, watching the ways of the men and women around you, can you set your sternward gaze on Him—*and wait?* Can you physically turn on the boat bench, throw your legs to the other side, and quietly study the contours of His face in the night? Can you call down deep for courage in His presence, waiting for Him to awake and affect His plans; can you believe in darkness what you claimed to believe by day?

Do you believe in Jesus?

Do you believe in Jesus—*right now?*

For imagine that suddenly, starting, He has shaken Himself awake, out of His back-of-the-boat sleep, and He rises to seated upon that cushion. Curious, He watches all the chaos—wind, water, waves—and then He's watching all the movements of the others. Their shouting, crying, bailing, wailing. Their seeming answers to the chaos, pandemonium, fear.

Now He has locked eyes with you. You are, bow to stern, totally engaged with Him.

And even amidst the sounds of storm, splashing, tearing, banging, screaming, howling, crashing, you can hear what He says to you: *"I will never fail you. I will never abandon you."*

And His eyes ask: *Do you believe Me?*

About Eugene Luning

Eugene Luning directs *The Union*, a ministry of teaching, speaking, retreats, podcasting and spiritual counseling. His overriding passion is speaking of Jesus.

Eugene graduated from Westmont College in Santa Barbara, California, and, before that, received his preparatory education at John Burroughs School in St. Louis, Missouri. Prior to his work with The Union, Eugene syndicated commercial real estate transactions in California and the Midwest, and also served for a number of years with the youth ministry, Young Life.

Eugene and his wife, Jenny, are the parents of three children, Hadley, Tripp, and Hoyt. They live in Colorado Springs, Colorado.

Notes

Notes

Notes

Notes

Experience a personal revival!

Spirit-empowered content from today's top Christian authors delivered directly to your inbox.

Join today!
lovetoreadclub.com

Inspiring Articles
Powerful Video Teaching
Resources for Revival

Get all of this and so much more, e-mailed to you twice weekly!

LOVE TO READ CLUB
by **D** DESTINY IMAGE

Made in the USA
Coppell, TX
01 June 2020

26795141R00095